Armed & Victorious

An Extensive Study on the Armor of God

Michelle M. Woodruff

ISBN 0-7414-4640-5

Edited by Keta Evans

Cover design by Tom Moeung

Published by:

INFINITY
PUBLISHING.COM

1094 New DeHaven Street, Suite 100
West Conshohocken, PA 19428-2713
Info@buybooksontheweb.com
www.buybooksontheweb.com
Toll-free (877) BUY BOOK
Local Phone (610) 941-9999
Fax (610) 941-9959

Printed in the United States of America

Printed on Recycled Paper

Published May 2008

~ Dedication ~

I lovingly dedicate this book
to my Heavenly Father.
Thank you for entrusting me with
Your message.

~ Acknowledgements ~

My heartfelt thanks to:

Keta Evans

Thank you for hundreds of hours of selfless service!

"God is fair; He will not forget
the work you did and the love you showed
for Him by helping His people."
(Hebrews 6:10)

Joey, Jonathan and Jessica

Thank you for bringing such joy to my life
And laughter to my heart!
You three are my greatest accomplishments!

"Children are a gift from the Lord;
they are a reward from him."
(Psalms 127:3)

My daughter-in-law Destiny

Thank you for being a wonderful wife to my son,
a dear sister to Jon & Jess and
a precious daughter to me!

"She is far more precious than jewels and her value is far above rubies and pearls."
(Proverbs 31:10b)

My husband Gefory

Thank you for being God's gift to me and my biggest fan!

"For I have derived great joy and comfort
and encouragement from your love..."
(Philemon Verse 7)

~ Contents ~

Foreword

Imagine for a moment an intense battle that is being fought on the frontlines. The sound of raging war and steady gunfire all around and right in the middle of all that is going on is a soldier. This soldier has to depend on his training, everything he has learned about his gear and how to conduct himself in battle. He not only needs the proper equipment to survive but also needs to understand how to use them. It is what is going to give him a chance to live and fight another day.

In our society today, the battle lines have been drawn. The battle for our marriages, families, and communities is being fought and like that soldier on the battlefield who needs the proper equipment and training to survive, Christians need to understand that God has equipped us for battle. Ephesians 6:12-13 states, "*We fight not against flesh and blood, but against principalities, against powers, and the rulers of the darkness of this age, against spiritual hosts of wickedness in the heavenly places. Therefore take up the whole armor of God, that you may be able to withstand... (NKJV).*"

We are not to engage the enemy exposed and vulnerable. No, we are to fit ourselves with the spiritual armor given to us by God that will enable us to walk in victory.

In this book, Michelle Woodruff, has literally provided us with a manual on the armor of God. Think of it as our basic training for Christians. Michelle has done an excellent job at defining every part of the armor and how we can apply it to our daily lives. **Armed and Victorious** will walk every Christian through a step-by-step process in which they can begin to fully understand their spiritual armor. From chapter to chapter, **Armed and Victorious** enables the reader to literally become a more effective soldier for the kingdom of God as they grow in knowledge and understanding. Applying the truth and principles in this book to your life will cause you to live a life of victory. Remember, you are called to be **Armed and Victorious!**

George Molina
Senior Pastor of Lifeway Church
www.lifewaychurchaz.com

Introduction

Throughout scripture we see a picture of mankind being dominated and held captive by sin's ugly clutches. The apostle Paul goes into great detail describing this picture in his letter to the Christians in Rome. In the third chapter of Romans Paul quotes the psalmist saying:

"As it is written, 'There is none righteous, no, not one; there is none who understands; there is no one who seeks after God. They have all turned aside; they have together become unprofitable; There is none who does good, no, not one. Their throat is an open tomb; with their tongues they have practiced deceit; the poison of asps is under their lips; whose mouth is full of cursing and bitterness. Their feet are swift to shed blood; destruction and misery are in their ways; and the way of peace they have not known. There is no fear of God before their eyes." (Psalms 14:1-3; Psalms 53:1-3)

Because of sin's control over mankind there wasn't a single person who could stand righteous before the living God. No one understood nor did any seek after God. In fact we did the opposite, we turned away from God and followed our own pursuits. Because of this we became unprofitable and unproductive in all our ways. We may have done random acts of kindness now and then but not without an ulterior motive or hidden agenda. We spoke lies and uttered deceit and our mouths were full of cursing and bitterness. Destruction and misery marked our path yet we still continued on our way searching for the peace we so deeply longed for. Having no fear or respect for God we blamed Him for the havoc our choices created. Yet even at our worse, sinners hating and cursing God, God still loved us.

In the book of Isaiah God responds to this wayward condition of man by declaring to us that it wasn't His ear that was deaf to our cries. On the contrary, it was man who had turned a deaf ear to God. It wasn't that God's arm was too short that He couldn't reach out and rescue us. We were the ones who refused to take hold of His outstretched hand. Our guilt separated us from God and our sinful condition separated us from His presence. Isaiah continues to say that it was our own sin that testified against us declaring that we knowingly departed from God. *(See Isaiah 59:1-5)*

This is the scene laid out before God. As He views the state of mankind and sees the condition of His creation, God is grieved. He trembles with displeasure at the devastation sin has brought upon man. He looked for justice but there was no man who could pay the price. He searched for one who would intercede on behalf of His creation, but there was none.

Therefore scripture tells us that His own arm brought salvation for Him, and His own righteousness sustained Him. God clothed Himself with His armor coming to the defense of His greatest love. Armed with His own righteousness as a breastplate and His own salvation as a helmet, He donned on the garments of vengeance. Justice would be served and fury would be poured out upon His adversaries. *(See Isaiah 59:16-17)*

Indeed God did demonstrate His love for us even while we were yet sinners. *(See Romans 5:8)*

"For at the proper time God sent His only begotten son, Jesus Christ, born of a woman and subject to the law, in order to redeem all who were under that law." (Galatians 4:4)

God didn't send His son Jesus to this world to condemn you and I, He sent Jesus so that through Him we might be delivered from sins' dominating hold upon us. *(See John 3:17)* Jesus came and through the cross He conquered Satan, totally disarming him and all his demons, stripping them of all power and authority over those who have put their trust in Jesus Christ as Lord and Savior. *(See Colossians 2:15)*

The book of Zechariah gives us a beautiful picture of removing the cloak of Satan's power and dominion over us and the placement of God's power and authority upon us.

"And the Lord said to Satan, 'The Lord rebuke you, Satan! The Lord who has chosen {place your name here} rebuke you! Is this not a brand plucked from the fire?' Now {place your name here} was clothed with filthy garments, and was standing before the Angel. Then He answered and spoke to those who stood before Him, saying, 'Take away the filthy garments from him.' And to him He said, 'See, I have removed your iniquity from you, and I will clothe you with rich robes." (Zechariah 3:2-4)

Isaiah defines those 'rich robes' in Isaiah chapter 61 verse 10:

"I will greatly rejoice in the Lord, My soul shall be joyful in my God; For He has clothed me with the garments of salvation, He has covered me with the robe of righteousness."

All power and authority has been given to Jesus who in turn has given us that same power and authority in His name. Through our relationship with Jesus Christ, we have been made God's ambassadors on this earth. *(See 2 Corinthians 5:20)* We are Christ's own personal representatives acting on His behalf. As an ambassador to a foreign land {for we are not of this world} we have been granted diplomatic immunity. Jesus told his disciples in the Gospel of Luke that He has given us {those who believe in the Lord Jesus Christ} all authority. Therefore nothing shall by any means hurt us. *(See Luke 10:19)*

The purpose of this study is to help you understand who you are in Christ and who Christ is in you. God armed

Himself to do battle with the enemy, and He has passed down His armor to us. This armor is given that we may successfully stand against the attacks of the enemy, walking a victorious productive life to the glory of God.

"But thanks be to God, who gives us the victory through our Lord Jesus Christ." (1 Corinthians 15:57)

The battle has been fought and the enemy has been conquered. This glorious victory has been handed over to you and I. We have been made more than conquerors and have gained a surpassing victory through the death and resurrection of the Lord Jesus Christ. *(See Romans 8:37)* As soldiers in God's army we are both **ARMED AND VICTORIOUS!**

"For You have armed me with strength for the battle;
You have subdued under me
those who rose against me."
(2 Samuel 22:40)

Chapter One

A Call  *To Arms*

"Finally, my brethren, be strong in the Lord and in the power of His might. Put on the whole armor of God, that you may be able to stand against the wiles of the devil. For we do not wrestle against flesh and blood, but against principalities, against powers, against the rulers of the darkness of this age, against spiritual hosts of wickedness in the heavenly places. Therefore take up the whole armor of God, that you may be able to withstand in the evil day, and having done all, to stand." (Ephesians 6:10-13)

The apostle Paul is writing this letter to the Christians in Ephesus from the confines of a prison cell in Rome. Looking out from his cell, Paul could see the Roman soldiers guarding him. Studying the armor they wore he began to understand that we too are heavily armed soldiers. However instead of being enlisted in the Roman army, taking orders from a Roman Centurion, we are enlisted in God's army receiving our direction and instruction from God Himself. As Paul concludes this letter, he reminds them to draw their strength from God and to rely upon His power and might. That ruling power which was on the inside of them the moment they received Jesus Christ as Lord and Savior. He then instructs them to put on the whole armor of God, that protective covering which gives them the ability to deflect the onslaught of the enemy. God's proven armor will enable the Christian to stand up against the strategies and deceits of the devil. For this same ruling power not only brought stability to their lives, it gave them the strength to stand upright in the midst of adversity. As a heavily armed soldier arrayed in God's armor, we stand immovable and unshakeable in the face of the enemy.

Paul explains to the fellow believers in Ephesus that our battle is not with flesh and blood. We are not wrestling with one another, but we struggle against Satan and all his cohorts. We know that we cannot enter a hand-to-hand combat with the enemy, throw him off balance and take him down in a wrestling match.

"For though we walk in the flesh, we do not war according to the flesh. For the weapons of our warfare are not carnal but mighty in God..." (2 Corinthians 10:3-4)

The word *'warfare'* is derived from the Greek word *'stratos'* which means to strategize. Our spiritual warfare is to be strategically planned out. As with any army preparing for war, we must first come up with a line of attack or a battle plan prior to entering the battle. Our enemy is no different. The devil strategically plans a line of attack, using methods that he has carefully thought out and an approach that will best carry out his assault against us.

What you and I must understand, however, is that our warfare or strategy is not derived from our natural abilities but comes from listening to and obeying the Holy Spirit. His strategy is far superior to any schemes or devices the devil chooses. Remember, the Holy Spirit always holds the key to victory. It is His desire to provide us with divinely inspired strategies that will defeat the works of the devil every time.

No successful commander would consider entering the battlefield without a plan of action. Even with an arsenal of weapons and artillery at their disposal, an army lacking great leadership with a strategic plan of attack will fail. A great leader knows the tactics of the enemy he sends his army to war against. God, having defeated our enemy, has provided you and I with the spiritual weapons necessary to successfully carry out His divinely inspired strategies.

For this reason Paul tells us that we must take up the complete armor of God. In order to successfully stand up against the enemy we must:

- Put on the belt of truth; which is the knowledge of the truth of God's Word.
- Put on the breastplate of righteousness; which represents a holy character obedient to the truth of the gospel of Jesus Christ.
- Cover our feet with the preparation of the gospel of peace; having both an eagerness and a willingness to advance against the devil bringing the good news of peace and reconciliation to God with every step we take.
- Take up the shield of faith; taking God at His Word by believing His promises and extinguishing every fiery dart of doubt and unbelief.
- Put on the helmet of salvation; which is that covering of protection, healing, soundness and wholeness.
- Take up the sword of the spirit, which is the Word of God.
- And we must pray and be alert, having a direct line of communication with our Commander-in-Chief.

To successfully stand against the enemy, Paul tells us that we must take up each of these seven pieces of armor God has provided. If our armor is incomplete in any one of these areas, we will be ineffective both offensively and defensively.

"For we do not wrestle against flesh and blood, but against principalities, against powers, against the rulers of the darkness of this age, against spiritual hosts of wickedness in the heavenly places." (Ephesians 6:12)

Wrestling during the first century was far different than the wrestling of today. It was an extremely violent and bloody sport with no rules, no guidelines, no time limits, and definitely no padded mats to soften the impact of being thrown down. Wrestling matches in that day were to the death. Fighters would rather die than walk out of the ring defeated and humiliated. These wrestlers were allowed to use any tactics imaginable to bring their enemy down. Strangling, choking, breaking fingers and ribs, gashing the face and gouging out the eyes were all acceptable. Whatever means necessary to take down the enemy and destroy his life was permissible.

When Paul compared our spiritual warfare to the enemy wrestling with us, he wanted us to realize that the devil is serious in his attempts to destroy us. It was Paul's intent to help believers realize that this conflict could be fierce. If we do not prepare ourselves spiritually to put a stop to such attacks, we will find ourselves in a wrestling match that we were never meant to be in.

"{For this reason you must} take up the whole armor of God, that you may be able to stand in the evil day, and having done all, to stand. Stand therefore, having girded your waist with truth, having put on the breastplate of righteousness, and having shod your feet with the preparation of the gospel of peace; above all, taking the shield of faith with which you will be able to quench all the fiery darts of the wicked one. And take the helmet of salvation, and the sword of the Spirit, which is the word of God; praying always with all prayer and supplication in the Spirit, being watchful to this end with all perseverance and supplication for all the saints." (Ephesians 6:13-18)

It is imperative we understand that Paul is trying to convey to us that there is a vast difference between wrestling and standing. The word 'wrestle' is defined as being "*a contest between two in which each endeavors to throw the other, and which is decided when the victor is able to hold his opponent down with his hand upon his neck".*[i] If we are wrestling with the sole objective being to pin our enemy down, we have forfeited two of the most important pieces of armor. We cannot possibly be holding onto our shield and sword if our hands are upon our enemy's neck. We would have had to lay those particular pieces of armor down in order to enter into a wrestling match with the enemy.

Notice that Paul stresses putting on the whole armor of God so that we may be able to stand. Now the meaning of the word 'stand' here means to "*make a stand, to make firm, to uphold or sustain the authority or force of anything, to stand immovable; one who does not hesitate or waver.*"[ii] Webster's definition of the word stand is "*to support oneself on the feet in an erect position; to maintain one's position, stand firm.*"[iii]

Wrestling the enemy is not the military stance God would have us take. Notice once Paul explains about putting on the full armor of God and describes the pieces of that armor, he never mentions wrestling again. Now that's not to say that we will never have difficulties or trials and temptations. This is the devil's world, but the Church is conquering and occupying new ground every day. As soldiers we are marching *to* a victory and *from* a victory. Jesus conquered Satan at the cross and we are living in that victory. Temptations will come and trials are inevitable. The enemy will continue to attack us trying to lure us into a wrestling match with him. But remember the words of Jesus:

"In the world you will have tribulation; but be of good cheer, I have overcome the world." (John 16:33)

In the Amplified Bible, which is an expanded translation, this verse reads:

"In the world you have tribulation and trials and distress and frustration; but be of good cheer [take courage; be confident, certain, undaunted]! For I have overcome the

world. [I have deprived it of power to harm you and have conquered it for you.]" (John 16:33)

God provided heavenly armor so that we may effectively stand, not wrestle, but stand against the enemy. Remembering this enemy has been disarmed and stripped of all power and authority over us. *(See Colossians 2:15)* As we clothe ourselves with the battle proven armor used to defeat the devil at Calvary, we are a reminder to him and his demons that they no longer have power, dominion, or authority over us. As we resist the devil the way God intended he will flee from us in defeat.

Nehemiah understood this principle very well. You will find his story in the Old Testament book of Nehemiah. He is a man employed by King Artaxerxes. During his service to the king he receives word from home that all is not well. The protective walls that once stood around his beloved city now lay in ruins. The city is war torn and devastated beyond belief. Nehemiah is heartbroken, not only over the condition of his homeland but for the people he so dearly loved. When the king sees how disturbed Nehemiah is over this situation he gives him the authority and provisions to repair the broken down city.

Preparations for the journey are made and Nehemiah is quickly on his way. However, there were those in the surrounding territories who were strongly opposed to the rebuilding of Jerusalem. These enemies of the people were angry and ridiculed the Jews telling them all the reasons why they couldn't accomplish the task set before them. But the work continued making the enemies' anger so intense that:

"They all plotted together to come and fight against Jerusalem, to injure and cause confusion and failure in it." (Nehemiah 4:8 Amp)

When word of the plot came to Nehemiah the people prayed to God and set watchman around the wall day and night. Everyone involved in the building of the walls worked with one hand while holding a weapon in the other. Because the work was so great workman were scattered in various places throughout the wall. As part of their defense against the enemy Nehemiah told the workers that no matter where they were positioned on the wall, when they heard the trumpet blast they were to converge to that area with their swords drawn ready to come to the assistance of their brother in need.

"Those who built the wall and those who bore burdens loaded themselves so that everyone worked with one hand and held a weapon with the other hand. And every builder had his sword girded by his side, and so worked. And he who sounded the trumpet was at my side. And I said to the nobles and officials and the rest of the people, 'The work is great and scattered, and we are separated on the wall, one far from another. In whatever place you hear the sound of the trumpet, rally to us there, Our God will fight for us." (Nehemiah 4:17-20)

When the enemy was spied, the trumpet sounded and the workers came running. It was there that they stood their ground, swords drawn ready to face down the enemy.

"And when our enemies heard that their plot was known to us and that God had frustrated their purpose, we all returned to the wall, everyone to his work." (Nehemiah 4:15)

When the enemy heard that their plot had been exposed and realized that God had frustrated their plans they retreated in defeat. Nehemiah and the residents of Jerusalem never fought, they simply stood their ground with swords drawn. They believed God's Word and trusted that He truly would fight for them. They realized that the battle belonged to God and that He was more than able to defeat the enemy. With the '*Call to Arms*' they rallied together taking their stand against the enemy.

Like Nehemiah, we too are called to a specific purpose. There is much work to be done in building the Kingdom of God. We too are both laborer and soldier, working with one hand, and holding our weapon in the other. We must be about our Father's business. Therefore, not only must the tools of our trade be sharpened and always at hand, but so must be the weapons of our warfare.

As in the days of Nehemiah, we too have an enemy who is enraged over the progress we are making. The enemy plots against us with the intention of causing injury, confusion and failure. In the Gospel of John, Jesus calls him a thief who comes to steal, kill and destroy. *(See John 10:10)* However, unlike Nehemiah, our enemy is not a physical one. He is not made of flesh and blood but is spirit and must be dealt with in the spirit. Because of this we must use the weapons God has provided us. Even though Jesus has already defeated him, stripping and disarming him and his demons of all power and dominion, he still continues to plot against us trying to thwart God's plan for our lives. He is determined to convince us that we do not have the power and authority God has given us through Jesus.

For this reason you and I must put on the full armor of God, understanding the significance of each piece. It is imperative that we understand that as with any soldier, donning our armor everyday is necessary if we are to stand in the victory of Christ. Through the apostle Paul, God has given us a '*Call to Arms*'. Will you answer His call?

"I heard the voice of the Lord saying:
'Whom shall I send, and who shall go for Us?'
Then I said, 'Here am I! Send me!"
(Isaiah 6:8)

Chapter Two

The Belt  of Truth

"Therefore take up the whole armor of God, that you may be able to withstand in the evil day, and having done all, to stand. Stand therefore [hold your ground], having tightened the belt of truth around your loins..." (Ephesians 6:13-14 Amp)

God has provided you and I with the weapons that will protect and defend the victorious life God has granted us. Even though our enemy is not of flesh and blood, he is very real. Each piece of armor that God has handed down to us is significant and vital to our successful stance against the enemy.

The first piece of armor that we are to take up is the belt of truth. Scripture tells us that truth is to be fastened securely around our loins. The word 'loins' means that place where life resides. Our life must be founded on the truth of the gospel of Jesus Christ. We cannot afford to rely upon our own strengths and abilities but must lean entirely upon God in absolute trust and confidence. This confident trust in God's Word is a direct threat against the devil. Therefore, he will attempt to shake our confidence and destroy our trust with the hopes of blinding us to God's truth. In Paul's second letter to the Christians in Corinth he states that:

"...The god of this world has blinded the minds of them which believe not, lest the truth of the glorious gospel of

Jesus Christ, who is the image of God should shine upon them." (2 Corinthians 4:4)

In the previous chapter we learned that Satan is a thief who comes to steal, kill and destroy. From the beginning of time Satan has tried to steal the truth from the heart of God's people. He manipulates God's word with the intention of casting doubt in the hearts and minds of people as to whether or not God truly meant what he said.

Adam and Eve are an example of a trust that was stolen and almost destroyed. The book of Genesis gives the account of God giving Adam complete stewardship over all creation. Adam had authority and dominion over every living thing, but with that authority also came responsibility as well as accountability.

"Then the Lord God took the man and put him in the Garden of Eden to tend and keep it. And the Lord God commanded the man, saying, 'Of every tree of the garden you may freely eat; but of the tree of the knowledge of good and evil you shall not eat, for in the day that you eat of it you shall surely die." (Genesis 2:15-17)

Satan, in the guise of a serpent, came to Eve and questioned God's authority denouncing the truth of His words.

"Now the serpent was more cunning than any beast of the field which the Lord God had made. And he said to the woman, 'Has God indeed said, 'You shall not eat of every tree of the garden'?" And the woman said to the serpent, 'We may eat the fruit of the trees of the garden; but of the fruit of the tree which is in the midst of the garden, God has said, 'You shall not eat it, nor shall you touch it lest you die." Then the serpent said to the woman, 'You will not surely die." (Genesis 3:1-4) [Revelation 12:9 reveals that the age-old serpent is the Devil and Satan]

Satan is very subtle and devious. He will question what God says and endeavor to make you wonder whether or not God can be trusted to do what He says He will do.

"God is not a man, that He should tell or act a lie, neither the son of man, that He should feel repentance for what He has promised. Has He said and shall He not do it? Or has He spoken and shall He not make it good?" (Numbers 23:19 Amp)

In the Old Testament book of Numbers, God tells Moses that His power and ability has not become inadequate or frustrated.

"...You shall see now whether My Word shall come to pass for you or not." (Numbers 11:23 Amp)

Eve chose the lies of the devil over the truth of God's word.

"So when the woman saw that the tree was good for food, that it was pleasant to the eyes, and a tree desirable to make one wise, she took of its fruit and ate. She also gave to her husband with her, and he ate. Then the eyes of both of them were opened, and they knew that they were naked; and they sewed fig leaves together and made themselves coverings. And they heard the sound of the Lord God walking in the garden in the cool of the day, and Adam and his wife hid themselves from the presence of the Lord God..." (Genesis 3:6-8)

Satan came with his trickery and deceit blinding the eyes of Adam and Eve to the truth of God's Word. They acted in disobedience and found that the consequence of their actions was not only physical death, but for the first time in their existence they would find themselves separated from God. No longer could they walk with Him in the cool of the evening, their sin had separated them from His presence. The glory that once covered them had departed and they found themselves naked and exposed in their sin. Now instead of longing for His presence they hid from Him in shame.

"Then the eyes of them both were opened, and they knew that they were naked; and they sewed fig leaves together and made themselves apron-like girdles. And they heard the sound of the Lord God walking in the garden in the cool of the day, and Adam and his wife hid themselves from the presence of the Lord God among the trees of the garden." (Genesis 3:7-8)

They came to the sobering realization that God was true to His Word. They were banished from the garden sent away in shame, yet they had hope in their heart because God had declared to them that He would send a Savior, a Redeemer that would deliver them from their sin.

Paul tells us that we must put on the belt of truth in order to successfully stand up against the strategies and deceits of the devil. We must know in whom we believe. The gospel of John tells us:

"In the beginning was the Word, and the Word was with God, and the Word was God. (John 1:1) And the Word became flesh and dwelt among us, and we beheld His glory, the glory as of the only begotten of the Father, full of grace and truth." (John 1:14)

In that same chapter John tells us that truth came through Jesus Christ. Jesus, Himself, states in the 14th chapter of John that He is truth.

"Jesus said to him, 'I am the way, the truth, and the life. No one comes to the Father except through Me." (John 14:6)

It is imperative that we know the truth, and are secure in that truth. For scripture tells us that:

"If you abide in My word, you are My disciples indeed. And you shall know the truth, and the truth shall make you free." (John 8:31-32)

In other words, if we are secure in our knowledge of who Jesus is and what He did, then the truth of that knowledge will free us from the dominion of sin. Satan will be powerless in our lives for he has no control over us. It is truth that will preserve you *(See Psalms 40:11)* and it is truth that will faithfully lead you in stability and reliability. *(See Psalms 25:5)*

The Roman soldiers guarding Paul understood the importance of the leather belt that made up part of their armor. This leather belt was worn around the waist and would hold most of the other pieces of their armor in place. Similarly, the other pieces of the Christian's armor depend on, and are held in place by, his spiritual *'belt'* or his knowledge of the *'truth'* of Scripture. We must come to the place in our walk with Jesus where we not only believe *in* God but also *believe* God. No doubts, no wavering, and no wrestling back and forth as to whether or not God meant what He said. God is truth. And it is this truth that will reveal who He is, what He has accomplished, and all He has promised to do in and through us.

In order for the rest of our spiritual armor to be effective, the belt of truth, God's Word, must be central in our lives. The moment you or I begin to neglect God's Word and stop applying it to our everyday lives', will be the exact moment we begin to lose our sense of righteousness and peace. The devil will start attacking our mind more and more in the attempt to fill it with his lies and vain imaginations. When we remove God's Word from its rightful place in our lives it won't be long before we begin to spiritually fall apart.

With our belt securely fastened and our hold on the truth just as secure, we are declaring to the enemy that sin's dominion over us has been severed. We know the truth, and it is this truth of the gospel of Jesus Christ that has freed us from Satan's crafty subtleties and lying deceits. We need not fight this battle the enemy has waged against us. We simply take our position, stand with absolute trust and confidence, and see the salvation of the Lord.

"You will not need to fight in this battle.
Position yourselves, stand still,
and see the salvation of the Lord, who is with you."
(2 Chronicles 20:17)

Chapter Three

The Breastplate 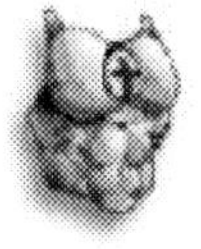 of Righteousness

"Stand therefore, having girded your waist with truth, having put on the breastplate of righteousness." (Ephesians 6:14)

In the previous chapter we saw how the apostle Paul compared the armor of the soldiers guarding him, with the spiritual armor God provided His church. Through this illustration we have learned to put on and surround ourselves with the truth of the gospel of Jesus Christ.

In preparation for facing the enemy, a Roman soldier would fasten his leather belt to his waist. Once this was secure, the soldier would then put on the breastplate attaching it to his belt.

Paul is instructing us to put on God's righteousness the same way a soldier puts on his breastplate. For in the same manner that a breastplate protects the heart physically, righteousness protects the heart spiritually.

We must understand however, that it is God's righteousness that we are putting on, not our own. Scripture tells us that:

"There is none righteous, no, not one." (Romans 3:10)

In fact, our righteousness is described in the book of Isaiah as being like filthy rags.

"For we have all become like one who is unclean and all our righteousness (our best deeds of rightness and justice) is like filthy rags or a polluted garment; we all fade like a leaf, and our iniquities, like the wind take us away [far from God's favor, hurrying us toward destruction]." (Isaiah 64:6 Amp)

Let's refer back to the prophet Zechariah's account for a better understanding of these filthy garments.

"Now Joshua was clothed with filthy garments, and was standing before the Angel. Then He answered and spoke to those who stood before Him, saying, 'Take away the filthy garments from him.' And to him He said, 'See, I have removed your iniquity from you, and I will clothe you with rich robes." (Zechariah 3:2-4)

Apart from Jesus our righteousness is nothing more than filthy rags. Because of our sinful nature, our righteousness could never equal God's. No matter how good we tried to be, we could never be good enough on our own. But scripture tells us that everyone who trusts in Jesus; who confidently surrenders to and firmly relies upon Him will be saved. *(See Romans 1:16 Amp)* King David tells us in the book of Psalms that we:

"*Receive righteousness from the God of our salvation.*" *(Psalms 24:5)*

The prophet Isaiah states:

"For He has clothed me with the garments of salvation, He has covered me with the robes of righteousness." (Isaiah 61:10)

As we call upon the name of the Lord Jesus, God removes the sin- covered garments we were clothed in and covers us with His garments of salvation. Upon receiving this salvation, we are then clothed in His robes of righteousness. Jesus, who knew no sin, became sin for us that we who were unrighteous might become righteous through Him.

"For He made Him who knew no sin to be sin for us, that we might become the righteousness of God in Him." (2 Corinthians 5:21)

In other words, we who were unrighteous have now become the righteousness of God in Christ Jesus.

Now the definition of the word 'righteousness' according to Webster's Dictionary is: *"to free from guilt or sin; as vindicated (set free, deliver; free from allegation or blame; to protect from attack or encroachment; defend)."*[iv] The meaning of the word 'defend' is: *"to drive danger or attack away from."*[v] Whereas the word 'encroachment' is defined as *"entering by gradual steps or by stealth into the possessions or rights of another."*[vi]

It is through the sacrificial blood of Jesus Christ that we have been freed from the guilt and penalty of sin. We have been vindicated; freed from accusations and allegations. It is God's righteousness that protects and drives away the attack of the enemy as he tries to encroach upon the territory God has already given us.

Remember, Paul tells us to put on God's complete armor in order to successfully stand against the strategies and deceits of the devil. Satan will try to stealthily enter our domain by taking gradual steps, so as not to be noticed, in order to steal, kill and destroy what God has graciously given to us. Because of this, it is essential that we arm ourselves with the righteousness of God. *(See Psalms 132:9)* For it is His righteousness that will protect us, defend us and go before us. God's righteousness is a covering of protection for us. It puts us in right standing before God, enabling us to possess a holy character that is obedient to the truth of the gospel of Jesus Christ.

It is imperative that we come to the understanding that Jesus is Truth, and that our righteousness is based upon that truth. It is the revelation that everything I have belongs to Jesus, everything I am is because of Him, and everything I do is through His power and authority. It is because of this truth, that we can stand in the face of the enemy in total victory. Armed with God's righteousness, we are declaring:

"*It is not by might, nor by power but by the Spirit of the Most High God". (Zechariah 4:6)*

We stand in confidence knowing that it is:

"No longer I that lives, but Christ that lives in and through me." (Galatians 2:20)

It is not about me any more. It is about Jesus. It is His truth that I surround myself with and it is His righteousness that I cover myself in.

Guilt and shame can no longer plague us. Failures and regrets can no longer pursue us. Condemnation can no longer haunt us because Jesus has cleansed us from all unrighteousness. He has removed the filthy garments of sin and has clothed us in His righteousness giving us the ability to be holy even as He is holy.

The apostle Paul in his second letter to the Christians in Corinth says:

"*If anyone is in Christ, he is a new creation; old things have passed away; behold all things have become new." (2 Corinthians 5:17)*

Then in his letter to the Ephesians he says:

"To put on the new nature (the regenerate self) created in God's image, (Godlike) in true righteousness and holiness." (Ephesians 4:24 Amp)

Paul is saying that we are to put off the old man or the old nature. The old ways of doing things and the old ways of responding are no longer acceptable. We must obey and submit ourselves to God's righteousness understanding that to seek to establish righteousness or a means of salvation on our own merits is futile. For the bible tells us that the righteousness of God comes by believing, with personal trust and confident reliance on Jesus. This righteousness is available to all who believe, there is no distinction.

"Since all of us have sinned and fallen short of the honor and the glory that God gives and receives." (Romans 3:23 Amp)

Jesus explains this very truth in the parable of the wedding feast found in the Gospel of Matthew in the twenty-second chapter.

In this parable Jesus describes a king whose son is about to be married. He sends out the wedding invitations not once, not even twice, but three times in hopes of finding those who were willing to come and be a part of this glorious celebration. The king held nothing back, all who attended the royal wedding were provided with the proper wedding garments.

However, there was one guest in particular who decided to respond to the invitation, but felt that he was good enough to come as he was. He refused the graciousness of the king by opting to wear his own garments rather than exchanging them for the robes of the kingdom. The gracious gift of the father had been spurned and rejected.

When the king learned of this, he became furious at the audacity and prideful attitude of this individual. Jesus told this story to illustrate the kingdom of heaven. God has sent forth the invitation providing all who accept with the garments of salvation and the robes of righteousness. To deny these garments, would be to forfeit the gifts they represented.

We must not be ignorant of the righteousness that God has so graciously and freely given to us. For this righteousness not only enables us to be acceptable to Him in word, thought and deed, but it empowers us with the ability to carry out His divine purpose for our lives. It is the righteousness of God, through Jesus Christ, that gives us the ability to stand and the power to continue standing victoriously even in the face of God's greatest enemy. Therefore, having put on the breastplate of righteousness, we stand.

"But rise and stand on your feet;
for I have appeared to you for this purpose,
to make you a minister and a witness both of the things
which you have seen and of the things
which I will yet reveal to you."
(Acts 26:16)

Chapter Four

The Shoes of the  *Gospel of Peace*

"Stand therefore, having girded your waist with truth, having put on the breastplate of righteousness, and having shod your feet with the preparation of the gospel of peace." (Ephesians 6:14-15)

The soldiers of Rome understood the importance of balance and positioning in combat. What might appear as insignificant to you and I was deemed a necessary and vital part of the soldier's armor. A soldier's footwear played a vital role in avoiding disaster. One misstep and the outcome could be fatal.

The Roman soldier altered his footwear to be functional in many ways. He needed a shoe that could be comfortably worn all day whether he were working, marching or standing for long periods of time. At the end of a long day though his feet would be aching there would be no blisters or sores. He could easily remove his sandals, dip his bare feet in the nearest river cooling them off and washing away the aches of the day. Refreshed, he was ready to continue on his way.

The underside of his sandal was designed to be fitted with iron hobnails or studs, similar to modern day athletic cleats.[vii] These nail-studded sandals were intended to offset the various countermeasures that an enemy might use to slow down his advance or to dislodge his footing during combat. So not only did this footwear protect the soldier's feet over rough terrain, it also allowed him to trample upon his fallen enemy as he advanced in battle.

As a prisoner of the Roman guard, Paul could understand the importance of balance and positioning in the Christian's life. He could also appreciate the significance of being prepared and ready. The midst of the battle is not the time to be donning your armor.

From his prison cell in Rome, Paul is penning his letter to the Christians in Ephesus explaining to them the necessity of being prepared.

"Stand therefore...having shod your feet in preparation [to face the enemy with the firm-footed stability, the promptness, and the readiness produced by the good news] of the Gospel of Peace." (Ephesians 6:14a & 15 Amp)

We have put on truth securing it in our heart. And we've armed ourselves with righteousness as one putting on his breastplate. Now Paul is instructing us to cover our feet in preparation for facing the enemy. He explains that God's peace is a covering that produces a firm-footed stability that not only instills a willingness to advance against the enemy, but the confidence to do so. It is God's peace upon which we stand and move. A peace that is defined as:

"That tranquil state of a soul assured of its salvation through Christ, fearing nothing." (Philippians 4:7 Amp)

Isaiah tells us that this peace from God is a by-product of walking and operating in God's righteousness.

"The effect of righteousness will be peace [internal and external], and the result of righteousness will be quietness and confident trust forever." (Isaiah 32:17 Amp)

Having our feet shod with the preparedness of the gospel of peace will enable us to walk and lead a life worthy of the divine calling to which you and I have been called.

The prophet Isaiah declares that we will run, and not be weary, we will walk, and not faint. *(See Isaiah 40:31)* In the book of Proverbs, King Solomon shares the wisdom God imparted to his father David.

"When you walk, your steps shall not be hampered [your path will be clear and open]; and when you run, you shall not stumble."(Proverbs 4:12)

In a prayer of thanksgiving by the prophet Habakkuk he declares:

"The Lord God is my Strength, my personal bravery, and my invincible army; He makes my feet like hinds' feet and will make me to walk [not stand in terror, but to walk] and make [spiritual] progress upon my high places [of trouble, suffering, or responsibility]."(Habakkuk 3:19 Amp)

To anyone familiar with the wild, they would understand that '*hind's (deer's) feet*' speaks of agility and endurance. A Roman soldier would depend upon his footwear to help him advance against his adversary in order to possess his enemy's territory. Likewise having our feet shod with the gospel of peace enables us to advance against our enemy, possessing territory that is rightfully ours through the power and authority of Jesus Christ. God has provided us with a firm-footed stability that allows us to walk in confidence. We also possess an enduring agility that enables us to make progress in our advancement against the enemy.

In the Old Testament God spoke to both Moses and Joshua promising them that:

"Every place on which the sole of your feet treads shall be yours." (See Deuteronomy 11:24; Joshua 1:3)

Having our '*feet shod*' implies standing and walking in God's power and authority. Scripture tells us that God orders our footsteps and every place our foot sets down, we possess for His kingdom. *(See Psalms 37:23)* Everywhere we walk we bring God's peace and reconciliation. We are His ambassador, acting on His behalf.

It was Paul's intention to help Christians understand that in the same manner that a Roman soldier used his footwear to trample the enemy, the gospel of peace enables us to trample upon our enemies. Jesus told his disciples in the gospel of Luke that He had given them:

"The power and the authority to trample upon serpents and scorpions and over all the power of the enemy." (Luke 10:19)

It is this power and authority that makes us a threat to the enemy. Intimidating him even more is our understanding of *how* to operate in this power and authority God has given us.

Satan knows that balance and positioning are important aspects to a Christian's life. Therefore, he will do whatever it takes to throw us off center, causing us to lose our footing and positioning. He will throw circumstances our way in hopes of destroying our faith. If that doesn't work he'll use weapons of discouragement by condemning us for our shortcomings and, or he'll bring temptations to try enticing us to sin.

There will be times when he will come at you hard and furiously. At other times he is subtle, perhaps even enticing with flattery. One moment he tells you you're not good enough to call yourself a Christian and you find yourself fighting guilt. Then he tells you you're a Super Christian and you find yourself battling a prideful attitude. One day he's trying to convince you that you're too weak to do what God is calling you to, and the next day he's trying to convince you that you're strong enough to go at it in your own power and strength.

How can you possibly keep up and combat all of these attacks? It's simple. We learn to allow God's peace to rule and reign in our heart.

"Let the peace from Christ rule (act as umpire continually) in your hearts [deciding and settling with finality all questions that arise in your minds.]..." (Colossians 3:15 Amp)

Again, we must remember Paul's advice to the Christians at the church in Corinth.

"For the weapons of our warfare are not physical weapons, but they are mighty before God for the overthrow and destruction of strongholds. [Inasmuch as we] refute arguments and theories and reasoning's and every proud and lofty thing that sets itself up against the true knowledge of God; and we lead every thought and every purpose away captive into the obedience of Jesus Christ." (2 Corinthians 10:4-5 Amp)

In Paul's letter to the Christians in Philippi, he explains to them that God's peace will keep their heart. *(See Philippians 4:7)* The word *'keep'* when translated from the original Greek language means '*shall guard'*. This was a military term for a sentinel standing guard duty.

At the same time they were reading the words of Paul, there was a Roman garrison guarding the City of Philippi. These citizens were accustomed to seeing soldiers protecting their city from a possible hostile invasion. Because of this, the recipients of Paul's letter could truly understand the significance of God's peace guarding their heart. They not only understood that God's peace ruled their heart; they also knew His peace would guard and protect it as well.

In the book of Isaiah, God gives a promise to everyone who will determine to keep his mind stayed and fixed upon the Lord his God.

"You will guard him and keep him in perfect and constant peace whose mind [both its inclination and its

character] is stayed on You, because he commits himself to You, leans on You, and hopes confidently on You." (Isaiah 26:3 Amp)

Having God's peace in place in our lives gives us the assurance and the confidence we need to step out in faith and make those moves God is leading us to make. Without this powerful and mighty weapon operating in our lives, the enemy will attempt to kick, punch, pull, and distract us. But when God's victorious peace is firmly activated in our mind and emotions, we will have the ability to continue marching ahead, unaffected by the devil's attempt to take us down.

Having our *'feet shod'* with the gospel of peace implies standing and walking in God's power and authority. It speaks of preparation and possession. It also represents sonship.

Jesus explained this truth in the parable of the prodigal son. *(See Luke 15:11-23)* The story begins with the younger of two sons telling his father that he wanted what was rightfully his. He wanted his father's inheritance, but he didn't want to wait until his father died. That would take too long. He wanted his share of the money and he wanted it now. So the father gave his younger son his inheritance, and as soon as he got what he wanted he left in search of adventure and excitement. He traveled the world spending his money on frivolous things. Before he knew it his money disappeared, as well as his newly found friends. His entire fortune was wasted on reckless and loose living. He had nothing left of his father's inheritance. From riches to rags he soon found himself living on the streets eating garbage and food fit only for pigs. He'd lost everything. The shirt on his back, the shoes on his feet, the place he once called home – they were all gone. The relationship he'd spurned, the father he'd turned his back on, gone forever. Cold and lonely, disgraced and ashamed, the one who thought he had all the answers found himself facing starvation. In the depths of his despair he began to realize just how good things were for him when he was home. Even his father's servants were better clothed and fed than he. He realized there was nothing left to do but to return to his father's house and humbly ask for his forgiveness. There was no false hope of going back to the way things were, he would consider it a blessing if his father would accept him as a mere servant. At least he'd be able to take a bath, put on clean clothes and eat food that was actually fit for human consumption. And so his journey home began. However, the end of his journey was nothing like what he had imagined.

With every step he took, the weight of his guilt and shame became heavier and heavier. As he turned down the path that led to his father's house he could see a figure in the distance. It took only seconds for the son to realize the figure was running towards him, or was he running at him. Fear gripped his heart as he realized it was his father. He didn't see a weapon in his father's hand, though he deserved to be stoned for the disrespectful way he treated his father.

"But while he was still a long way off, his father saw him and was moved with pity and tenderness for him; and he ran and embraced him and kissed him fervently. And the son said to him, Father, I have sinned against heaven and in your sight; I am no longer worthy to be called your son [I no longer deserve to be recognized as a son of yours]. But the father said to his bond servants, Bring quickly the best robe (the festive robe of honor) and put it on him; and give him a ring for his hand and sandals for his feet." (Luke 15:20-23)

This story ended differently than the younger son anticipated. Instead of condemnation and rejection, he received forgiveness and acceptance. Instead of a death sentence he received a pardon, and instead of disgrace and shame he was his father's pride and joy.

The filthy rags he came home in were quickly replaced with a robe that depicted his right standing. Hands once smooth and manicured were now hard and calloused. Yet his father didn't hesitate to slip the family crest upon his finger giving him all the authority of a son, a rightful heir.

Feet that were bare except for the shame and disgrace that covered them were quickly clad with sandals that also represented sonship.

You see the custom of that day permitted only the sons or the daughters of the father to be clad in sandals. Servants wore no sandals. Those in mourning, those who were a disgrace, and those who brought shame went barefoot as a sign of their place in society.

The father wanted all to see that his son had come home and that he was welcomed and made to be in right standing with the family. From the clothes on his back to the shoes on his feet, each depicted the power and authority the son received in his father's name. From that moment everywhere the son went and everything he did was on behalf of his father. And everyone who dealt with the son knew they were dealing with the father.

As a soldier donning his footwear, we put on the gospel of peace, dispelling all doubt, fear and apprehension. A soldier who is worried, or unprepared for battle will easily fall at the hands of the enemy.

God prepares and arms us with the ability to advance against the enemy. The gospel of peace empowers us not only to take ground but also to crush the enemy in the process.

"And the God of peace will crush Satan under your feet shortly." (Romans 16:20)

The meaning of the word *'crush'* is to *'obliterate, smash, demolish, and reduce to nothing. It is the act of snapping, breaking, and crushing bones beyond recognition.'*[viii]

Now the word *'shortly'* actually comes from a military term that described the way the Roman soldiers would march in formation. The commanding officer would instruct his soldiers to lift their feet high and to stomp loud, warning everyone near that they were coming through town. Under no circumstances were these soldiers to slow down or get out of formation. They were instructed to ignore whatever obstacle was in their way. Whether it be the enemy standing in front of them or an innocent bystander fallen down in their path, they were to continue on. Stomping right over the top of them leaving the adversary or unfortunate person completely obliterated and trampled beyond recognition. Their orders were to continue marching, stomping, and pounding no matter what was in their path.

When the devil gets in our way attempting to hinder the fulfillment of God's Word in our lives, we are to lift our feet high, pound down as hard as we can, and stomp all over him as we march forward in victory. We have been equipped with the gospel shoes of peace enabling us to crush and bruise him beyond recognition. With God as our Captain, the devil has no chance of ever slipping out from under our heel.

When Jesus was victoriously raised from the dead, the devil was utterly smashed, crushed, and bruised. It is our God given mission to reinforce this victory already won.

We are to be committed to the mission of Jesus Christ. We have been called, equipped, and anointed and now we must go in the power and the authority given to us by God Himself. As it is written:

> *"How beautiful are the feet of those who preach the gospel of peace, who bring glad tidings of good things!"*
> *(Romans 10:15; Isaiah 52:7)*

Chapter Five

The Shield of Faith

"Above all, taking the shield of faith with which you will be able to quench all the fiery darts of the wicked one." (Ephesians 6:16)

The Roman Army was the most formidable of its time. A highly efficient and thoroughly professional body of soldiers, it was a mercenary force not to be reckoned with. These soldiers were well equipped and well trained. And for a time, they were Paul's constant companions.

In the midst of prison life, it is safe to surmise that Paul probably had ample opportunity to observe the soldiers in their daily activities. Perhaps he even observed a few of them training as they learned to skillfully use their armor and weaponry.

Thus far we have learned the significance of the soldier's belt, breastplate and shoes. Now Paul introduces the next piece of armor, the shield.

The shield of the Roman soldier was designed to protect him from spears and arrows thrown by the enemy. This massive 2½' wide by 4' high shield was made with heavy wooden planks glued together and then curved to fit the body. The soldier would cover these wooden planks with linen, animal skin and sometimes even metal. He would then anoint the shield's leather covering with oil thus making its' surface slippery and impregnable.

The Roman soldier would design his shield with this particular curvature so that any missiles thrown at him would be deflected to one side, usually the left. The soldier found that if his shield were flat, a rock or arrow hitting the shield would make a direct impact. This would mean the soldier's arms would have to absorb the brunt of the impact generated by the missile. Being curved, the shield would allow arrows and enemy blows to glance off without inflicting the full force of the impact onto the soldier sheltering behind it. It was imperative for the soldier to allow his shield to do the work for him, thus enabling him to reserve his energy and strength for the duration of the battle.

During this time in history, it was common practice to wrap the tips of arrows in linen, and then soak them in pitch. The tip of the arrow was then ignited and shot at the enemy. Upon impact, the arrow would shatter, scattering burning pieces several feet causing anything flammable to burst into flames. The most reliable protection against these flaming missiles was the shield. It's covering of leather, amply anointed with oil, would deflect and often times extinguish the fiery darts of the enemy.

Paul is comparing the Roman soldier's shield to that of our faith. Like the shield, our faith needs frequent anointings of the Holy Spirit. Without a fresh touch from God's Holy Spirit within our lives, we too will become brittle, hard and stiff. If you ignore your faith never allowing it to develop and never seeking a fresh anointing of God's Spirit, when challenges come your faith will not be soft and flexible, or pliable enough to endure the enemy's attack. A faith that is neglected almost always breaks and falls to pieces in the face of confrontation.

Satan has a quiver full of fiery darts. Discouragement, fear, doubt, insecurity, a whole array of emotions that can often times disable and destroy our effectiveness as followers of Christ. With this understanding, Paul writes:

"Above all, taking the shield of faith with which you will be able to quench all the fiery darts of the wicked one." (Ephesians 6:16)

Up until this point Paul's instructions are to *put on* the armor of God. Now he is telling Christians to *take up* the shield of faith.

In the Greek Dictionary of the New Testament the meaning of the word, 'taking' means '*to lift up; receive; take in; to get hold of with intensity.*'"[ix]

In his letter to the Ephesians, Paul says that it is imperative that we receive God's protective covering, taking hold of it with a firm grip and to lift it up above all else.

What exactly is this protective covering? This shield of faith, is it our faith that we are to lift up above all else? Before I answer this question, let's review what we have learned thus far.

We have put on the belt of truth acknowledging and accepting the truth of the gospel of Jesus Christ. Next, we've put on the breastplate of righteousness exchanging our sinful nature for Christ's sinless nature thus becoming the righteousness of God in Christ. We then put on the gospel shoes of peace, bringing with every step God's peace and reconciliation. Now since it is God's peace, God's righteousness and God's truth, why then would we think it is our faith?

You and I have each received a measure of faith, God's faith. Scripture tells us that we are:

"Crucified with Christ; nevertheless I live; yet not I, but Christ lives in me: and the life which I now live in the flesh I live <u>by the faith of the Son of God</u> who loved me, and gave himself for me."(Galatians 2:20 KJV)

In the 91st Psalm, King David declares God to be a refuge and a fortress to the believer. He further describes the protective covering God has provided us.

"He who dwells in the secret place of the Most High shall abide under the shadow of the Almighty. I will say of the Lord, "He is my refuge and my fortress; My God, in Him I will trust." Surely He shall deliver you from the snare of the fowler and from the perilous pestilence. He shall cover you with His feathers, and under His wings you shall take refuge; <u>His truth shall be your shield and buckler</u>." (Psalms 91:1-4)

The word *'truth'* as used in this particular passage is defined; *'faithfulness'*. In the Holman Christian Standard Bible this passage of scripture is translated:

"He will cover you with His feathers; you will take refuge under His wings. <u>His faithfulness will be a protective shield.</u>" (Psalms 91:4)

Above all else we are to lift up the shield of faith, that protective covering of God's faithfulness that deflects and extinguishes every fiery dart the enemy hurls our way. His is a faithfulness that reaches the very heavens, unchangeable and everlasting. His very name is Faithful!

"After that I saw heaven opened, and behold, a white horse [appeared]! The One who was riding it is called Faithful (Trustworthy, Loyal, Incorruptible, Steady) and True..." (Revelation 19:11 Amp)

The Webster's Dictionary defines *'faithful'* as '*worthy of trust; honest; loyal; reliable; dependable; accurate; exact; true.*'[x]

God is faithful, true to His Word. He cannot fail! Even when we are faithless God remains faithful!

"If we are faithless [do not believe and are untrue to Him], He remains true (faithful to His Word and His righteous character), for He cannot deny Himself." (2 Timothy 2:13 Amp)

God's faithfulness causes us to believe and trust God and His Word. This faith enables us to understand that God cannot lie, nor can He fail. He is God and His Word is settled in the heavens.

"Forever, O Lord, Your word is settled in heaven [stands firm as the heavens]. (Psalms 119:89 Amp)

It is also written:

"But the word of the Lord endures forever." (1 Peter 1:25)

Moses and the children of Israel knew firsthand what it was like to experience this faithful covering.

Their story begins in the book of Exodus. The children of Israel had been under Egyptian bondage for many years. The Israelites cried out to God because of their slavery and God heard their cries.

"Now it happened in the process of time that the king of Egypt died. Then the children of Israel groaned because of the bondage, and they cried out; and their cry came up to God because of the bondage. And the Lord said: "I have surely seen the oppression of My people who are in Egypt, and have heard their cry because of their taskmasters, for I know their sorrows. So I have come down to deliver them out of the hand of the Egyptians, and to bring them up from that land to a good and large land, to a land flowing with milk and honey." (Exodus 2:23; 3:7-8)

God saw the plight of His people and he sent a deliverer to them to bring them out from under the oppressive hand of the enemy. However, the Egyptian Pharaoh's heart was hardened towards God and he refused to allow God's people to go. After many plagues and much devastation, Pharaoh finally relented and allowed God's people to leave.

"Then Pharaoh called for Moses and Aaron by night, and said, "rise, go out from among my people, both you and the children of Israel. And go serve the Lord as you have said. Now it was told the king of Egypt that the people had fled, and the heart of Pharaoh and his servants was turned against the people; and they said, "Why have we done this, that we have let Israel go from serving us? And the Lord hardened the heart of Pharaoh king of Egypt, and he pursued the children of Israel;" (Exodus 12:31; 14:5 & 8)

Finally the Israelites had been freed from the bondage of their enemy. The burden was lifted from their backs and with a bounce in their step they head towards a land filled with promise and possibilities. I can just imagine the conversations and the laughter around the campfire that night as they shared with one another their dreams for the new life that lay ahead. Their lightheartedness is suddenly shattered with the realization that the distant thunder isn't a storm approaching, but the thunderous hooves of hundreds of horses and chariots coming after them.

"And when Pharaoh drew near, the children of Israel lifted their eyes, and behold, the Egyptians marched after them. So they were very afraid, and the children of Israel cried out to the Lord. And Moses said to the people, "Do not be afraid. Stand still, and see the salvation of the Lord, which He will accomplish for you today. For the Egyptians whom you see today, you shall see again no more forever. The Lord will fight for you, and you shall hold your peace." (Exodus 14:10; 14:13-14)

With the Red Sea before them and the Egyptian army behind them it looked as if the Israelites faced certain death, either by drowning or by the hand of an enraged enemy. But God's Word to the Israelites was to stand and see the salvation of the Lord. The battle was not theirs but God's alone. He would fight for them. He would deliver them. His faithfulness would be a protective covering both in front of them as well as behind them.

"And the Angel of God who went before the host of Israel moved and went behind them; and the pillar of the cloud went from before them and stood behind them. Coming between the host of Egypt and the host of Israel. It was a cloud and darkness to the Egyptians, but it gave light by night to the Israelites; and the one host came not near the other all night." (Exodus 14:19-20 Amp)

God's protective covering not only went before the Israelites but God became their rear guard as well. Unlike the Roman soldier's shield that protects only his front and left side, God's faithfulness protects us on every side. God declares this promise through the prophet Isaiah:

"For you will not go out with haste, nor will you go in flight [as was necessary when Israel left Egypt]; for the Lord will go before you, and the God of Israel will be your rear guard." (Isaiah 52:12 Amp)

The phrase *'rear guard'* is a military term used when part of the army or military force is detached from the main body and sent to guard the rear from surprise attack. God speaks to us through the prophet Isaiah telling us that it is His righteousness that shall go before us, and it is His glory that shall be our rear guard. But not only is God our rear guard, He is also our covering on the side not carrying the shield.

"The Lord is your keeper; the Lord is your shade on your right hand [the side not carrying a shield]." (Psalms 127:7 Amp)

God's faithfulness is all encompassing. Unlike the Roman soldier, we are not vulnerable. God's shield of faith is operating in our hearts and lives surrounding us with His faithfulness.

Through His death and resurrection the Lord Jesus Christ has imparted to us a measure of His faith. God's faith within us is an active force that motivates, urges and prompts us to fulfill God's divine purpose for our lives.

"For this very reason, adding your diligence [to the divine promises], employ every effort in exercising your faith to develop virtue (excellence, resolution, Christian energy), and in [exercising] virtue, [develop] knowledge (intelligence), and in [exercising] knowledge [develop] self-control, and in [exercising] self-control [develop] steadfastness (patience, endurance), and in [exercising] steadfastness [develop] godliness (piety), and in [exercising] godliness [develop] brotherly affection, and in [exercising] brotherly affection [develop] Christian love." (2 Peter 1:5-7 Amp)

It is through faith in Jesus that we are justified, sanctified and live an abundant life. And it is through this faith that we are shielded from the fiery darts of the enemy, and by which these fiery darts are extinguished.

God's faithfulness is a protective covering that we are to station in front of all the other parts of the armor. Apart from faith, the armor of God cannot adequately fulfill its' purpose. The belt of truth cannot function apart from faith in the truth. The breastplate of righteousness cannot operate apart from faith in the righteousness of Christ. The sandals of peace cannot effectively work aside from faith in the finished work of Christ. And as we shall soon learn, the helmet of salvation, the sword of the spirit and prayer all depend on faith. Scripture tells us:

"Without faith it is impossible to please Him." (Hebrews 11:6)

We take up the *'shield of faith'* by declaring God's faithfulness to His Word whenever we recognize Satan's lies. When Satan comes at us with his fiery darts of fear, we declare God's faithfulness by confessing His Word of truth that:

"God has not given us a spirit of fear, but of power and of love and of a sound mind." (2 Timothy 1:7)

When the fiery darts of doubt and unbelief are hurled at us, we proclaim God's faithfulness by declaring His truth that:

"All things are possible to him who believes." (Mark 9:23)

For example, when Satan hurls his fiery darts of sickness and disease, with confidence we can say of Christ that:

"He was wounded for our transgressions, He was bruised for our iniquities; the chastisement for our peace was upon Him, and by His stripes we are healed." (Isaiah 53:5)

Or when the enemy flings his fiery darts of discouragement trying to destroy our hopes and dreams we can lift up the shield of God's faithfulness and quench those fiery flames by declaring God's Word:

"The Lord does not delay and is not tardy or slow about what He promises..." (2 Peter 3:9a Amp)

Therefore let us:

"Lift up over all the covering shield of saving faith, upon which you can quench all the flaming missiles of the wicked one."(Ephesians 6:16)

For as it is written:

"He who promised is faithful."
(Hebrews 10:23b)

Chapter Six

The Helmet  *of Salvation*

"And take the helmet of salvation..."(Ephesians 6:17)

Rome controlled one of the greatest empires the world has ever seen, a monarchy of unified government, communication, and an invincible army of magnificently well-drilled soldiers whose discipline and weaponry proved far superior to others. Even though the Romans invented the majority of the weapons they used, they were always looking for ways to improve and advance their technology when facing the enemy. This was one of the reasons why the Roman army was so devastatingly effective. They were constantly embracing new weapons and techniques from the nations they conquered. After confiscating the weapons of their enemies, they would improve them technologically, thus creating an even greater weapon.

One such item of weaponry was the Roman helmet. The Romans would take the helmet of their fallen enemies, adapt it for themselves, and alter it to strengthen the areas of weakness detected in battle. Where other nations' created helmets made of cloth wrappings, animal hides or bones, the sophisticated technology of the Roman Empire allowed them to modify these designs and improve upon them by making their helmets out of iron or copper. Not only did the Roman helmet protect the soldier's head, but in expanding the design they created side guards that went down around the neck protecting it from potential blows of a sword, war club or battle-axe.

In battle, the two most vulnerable areas of attack are the heart and the head. These were the targets of the enemy. If a soldier is wounded in either of these places the end result was most likely death. For this reason, the helmet was as crucial a part of the soldier's armor as the breastplate. The head being the core of a soldier's ability to think, plan and wage war, his thinking ability was the most important factor in determining his victory or his defeat.

If a soldier went into battle unprepared and his head exposed, the fear of certain death would have already diminished his fighting ability making him an easy target for the enemy. We as Christians must be prepared with our minds focused and our thoughts lining up with God's Word, lest Satan deceive us with his lies. Scripture tells us that Satan comes to steal, kill and destroy. *(See John 10:10)*

If he can cause us to give up, quit, fall into despair, become discouraged or lose hope then he will have gained a victory in our lives. For this reason God has provided us with the necessary means to overcome every attack Satan brings against us.

"Put on the whole armor of God, that you may be able to stand against the wiles of the devil." (Ephesians 6:11)

God has provided us with His helmet of salvation. This is our protective covering of healing, soundness and wholeness that we may successfully stand against the wiles, strategies and deceitfulness of the enemy.

In Paul's letter to the Ephesians, he says we must take up the helmet of salvation. Notice he doesn't say to '*put on*' the helmet of salvation, but rather to '*take up*' the helmet of salvation. The word '*take*' here as defined in the Strong's Concordance means '*to grant access to*'.[xi] Webster's Dictionary defines the word '*helmet*' as a '*protective covering'.*[xii] So in essence Paul is telling us that because of the redemptive sacrifice of Jesus Christ, we have been granted access to the protective covering of God's salvation.

In another of Paul's writings he further explains this truth in his letter to the Christians in Thessalonica.

"But let us who are of the day be sober, putting on the breastplate of faith and love, and as a helmet the hope of salvation." (1 Thessalonians 5:8)

The phrase *'putting on'* as defined in Strong's Concordance means to *'sink into {be immersed] clothed'.*[xiii] Not only have we been granted full access to God's protective covering of salvation, we are to be totally immersed or clothed in it. Our mind, intellect and reasoning are covered by the saving knowledge of who Jesus Christ is and what He has done for us. This helmet of salvation protects us from a divided mind, a deceived mind, a doubtful mind and a discouraged mind.

Now the word *'hope'* as used in this passage has a different meaning than our modern day usage of the word. Many of us have made statements similar to 'Oh I hope it doesn't rain' or 'I hope I get that raise', yet both statements contain an uncertainty about an outcome of which we have no control. However, the biblical usage of the word hope denotes a different meaning entirely. According to the Strong's Concordance the word *'hope'* is defined as *'a joyful and confident expectation of eternal salvation.*[xiv] In other words, the biblical perspective of the word *'hope'* is an absolute. It is an unfailing expectation in the ability of our God to fulfill His promise to us.

The author of the Book of Hebrews describes God's hope as an anchor of the soul, both sure and steadfast. *(See Hebrews 6:19)* God's hope provides us with an anchor, something our intellect, emotions and reasoning's can hold onto.

The helmet of salvation enables the believer to maintain total confidence in victory, no matter how long the battle may seem to last. It empowers us to see beyond where we are to the bigger picture – the fulfillment of God's promises.

For the believer, salvation begins with a change of mind when we repent. The word '*repent*' as defined in the Amplified Bible means to *'think differently; change your mind, regretting your sins and changing your conduct.' (See Matthew 3:2 Amp)* Our Christian life grows as our mind is transformed and renewed.

"And do not be conformed to this world, but be transformed by the renewing of your mind, that you may prove what is that good and acceptable and perfect will of God." (Romans 12:2)

God's desire is for us to grow in the grace and knowledge of the Lord Jesus Christ, walking according to His Spirit and not according to our flesh.

"There is therefore now no condemnation to those who are in Christ Jesus, who do not walk according to the flesh, but according to the Spirit. For the law of the Spirit of life in Christ Jesus has made me free from the law of sin and death. For what the law could not do in that it was weak through the flesh, God did by sending His own Son in the likeness of sinful flesh, on account of sin: He condemned sin in the flesh, that the righteous requirement of the law might be fulfilled in us who do not walk according to the flesh but according to the Spirit. For those who live according to the flesh set their minds on the things of the flesh, but those who live according to the Spirit, the things of the Spirit. For to be carnally minded is death, but to be spiritually minded is life and peace. Because the carnal mind is enmity against God; for it is not subject to the law of God, nor indeed can be. So then, those who are in the flesh cannot please God."(Romans 8:1-8)

In order for us to live according to God's Spirit, we must set our minds on the things of the Spirit. In other words, our focus must be on God, and His perfect will for our lives. Paul stated it perfectly in his letter to the Philippians:

"Finally, brethren, whatever things are true, whatever things are noble, whatever things are just, whatever things are pure, whatever things are lovely, whatever things are of good report, if there is any virtue and if there is anything praiseworthy – meditate on these things." (Philippians 4:8)

Though the battle belongs to the Lord, we are still in a battle. Why else would God provide us with the spiritual weaponry to defeat the enemy in our lives? What we must understand is that God never told us to 'slay' the dragon. Remember, God has already defeated and stripped the enemy of all power and authority over Christians. He has been declared powerless in our lives. Our responsibility is to simply stand in the victory Christ has already won on our behalf. The '*battle belongs to the Lord' (See 1 Samuel 17:47b)* simply means the victory is His.

In his second letter to the Christians in Thessalonica, Paul tells them not to be *'shaken in mind, or be troubled'. (See 2 Thessalonians 2:2)* The Strong's Concordance defines the word *'shaken*[xv] as a comparison to a storm with high winds and waves; thoughts or words that agitate or shake you to the core causing you to totter or be overthrown. It also means to quake with fear and trembling. The phrase '*in mind'* denotes separation, departing or fleeing.[xvi]

Paul is instructing them not to allow thoughts contrary to God's Word to separate them from the truth of the Gospel of Jesus Christ. If we allow ourselves to give place to thoughts and imaginations that are contrary to the truth of God's Word, then we will be shaken in our stance against the enemy. It all goes back to Paul's admonition to think only on those things that are pleasing and acceptable to God.

"Finally, brethren, whatever things are true, whatever things are noble, whatever things are just, whatever things are pure, whatever things are lovely, whatever things are of good report, if there is any virtue and if there is anything praiseworthy – meditate on these things." (Philippians 4:8)

Let our heart's cry be that of King David:

"Let the words of my mouth and the meditation of my heart be acceptable in your sight O Lord, my strength and my Redeemer." (Psalms 19:14)

So what happens when Satan hurls words of doubt and unbelief at you or when he whispers words of defeat, discouragement, hopelessness and deception into your ear – how do you combat that?

"For though we walk in the flesh, we do not war after the flesh. For the weapons of our warfare are not carnal, but mighty through God to the pulling down of strongholds; <u>Casting down imaginations</u>, and every high thing that exalteth itself against the knowledge of God, and bringing into captivity every thought to the obedience of Christ." (2 Corinthians 10:3-5 KJV)

The phrase *'casting down'* as defined in the Strong's Concordance means, '*to pull down, demolish the subtle reasoning's of an opponent.* [xvii]

The word *'imaginations'* as depicted here in this passage means, *'A reasoning [thought, meditation, consideration, word) such as is hostile to the Christian faith.* [xviii]

The Strong's Concordance defines the word '*thought*' as being '*a mental perception; an evil purpose; a particular mode of thinking and judging.*'[xix]

The word '*capture*' in the above verse means '*to lead away captive; to remove; cause to cease; to take by force.*'[xx]

Paul is instructing us to cast down or demolish any word, thought, or purpose that would elevate itself over God's rightful place in our lives. Any thought, word or feeling that is hostile to the Christian faith is to be taken by force and led away to the place where it will cease to exist in our lives.

The apostle Peter tells us that we are to '*gird up the loins of our mind'. (See 1 Peter 1:13)* In other words we are to guard our thought life. Do not allow any thoughts to take up residence within our mind, intellect or reasoning that would be hurtful and destructive in our lives.

"Therefore, since Christ suffered for us in the flesh, arm yourselves also with the same mind, for he who has suffered in the flesh has ceased from sin." (1 Peter 4:1)

In the above verse, Peter states that we must arm ourselves with the mind of Christ, and if we are to cease from sin we must suffer or die to the flesh. How like human nature to want to shrink away from anything that has to do with suffering. Yet Scripture tells us that Jesus:

"Learned obedience through what He suffered." (Hebrews 5:8)

And it was that obedience that equipped Him to not only face the enemy but to conquer him as well. We too must embrace the sanctified experiences God allows us to go through that we also may learn the obedience that equips us for victory.

Faith is of the heart, whereas hope is of the mind. The helmet of salvation represents the protective covering for the mind of the saved person. Through the saving power of Jesus our mind is both transformed and renewed. Our mind becomes obedient to Christ as we take into captivity every thought and imagination contrary to His Word. The helmet of salvation enables us to take on a new attitude of holiness with thoughts of excellence rather than thoughts hostile to the Christian faith. As our minds remain steadfast we are kept in peace understanding that this salvation represents all that Christ has done for us.

"He saw that there was no one to intervene;
so His own arm worked salvation for Him, and
His own righteousness sustained Him,
He put on righteousness as His breastplate and
salvation as a helmet upon His head;"
(Isaiah 59:16-17)

Chapter Seven

The Sword of 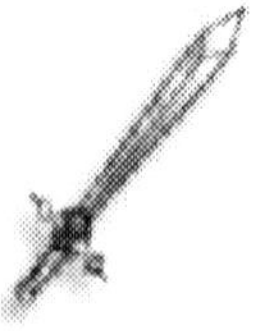 *the Spirit*

"And take the helmet of salvation, and the sword of the Spirit, which is the word of God;" (Ephesians 6:17)

The Roman Empire was one of the greatest military powers of their time. They conquered most of the civilized world by using superior weapons and tactics. The primary weapon of the Roman soldier was the Machiara sword. He would either live by it or die by it depending upon his effectiveness in using it.

This type of sword was both an effective and devastating weapon quite capable of severing a bronze helmet. The Machiara was unlike any other sword ever produced. Though its design was similar to that of the Spanish Celts it was different in the fact that it was very short, only 18 inches long versus 31 to 34 inches long. It was also different in the fact that not only was the point sharp, but both sides of the sword were sharpened as well. It was neither cumbersome nor heavy, but rather light weight and easily manipulated. It's look and size often deceived the enemy into thinking it was a substandard weapon. Oftentimes the enemy would laugh and taunt the Romans because of the seemingly short and inadequate swords they carried into battle. These barbarians surmised that they could win any fight because of the immense size of their sword. However, no matter which way the adversary would turn, they quickly found that the Roman soldier's sword was more versatile in penetrating their defenses. Because of its size and weight, the Roman soldier could easily cut one way and then the other making good use of its double-edged blade and sharp point. It wasn't long before the reputation of the Roman's sword struck terror into the hearts of their toughest foe.

In his letter to the Ephesians, Paul instructed them to:

"Take up the sword of the Spirit, which is the Word of God." (Ephesians 6:17)

In the original Greek text, it reads, *'take the Spirit as your Machiara Sword, that is the Word of God.* [xxi] Paul is likening the Word of God that the Spirit wields to that of the double-edged Machiara Sword that is both effective and devastating to its enemy.

The writer of Hebrews tells us that God's Word is alive. It is active and sharper than any two-edged sword that can penetrate and separate both spirit from soul and joint from marrow.

"For the Word that God speaks is alive and full of power making it active, operative, energizing and effective; it is sharper than any two-edged sword, penetrating to the dividing line of the breath of life and the immortal spirit, and of joints and marrow [of the deepest parts of our nature], exposing and sifting and analyzing and judging the very thoughts and purposes of the heart." (Hebrews 4:12 Amp)

Here again the Greek word for '*sword*' is *Machiara.* God's Word is an effective and devastating weapon when used against the enemy. How do we know this? Because this is the weapon Jesus used against Satan when tested and tried in the wilderness.

"Then Jesus was led up by the Spirit into the wilderness to be tempted by the devil. And when He had

fasted forty days and forty nights, afterward He was hungry. Now when the tempter came to Him, he said, "If You are the Son of God, command that these stones become bread." But He answered and said, "It is written, 'Man shall not live by bread alone, but by every word that proceeds from the mouth of God'." (Matthew 4:1-4)

One of the enemy's greatest tactics of defense is to try and instill doubt and confusion in the hearts and minds of man concerning what God has spoken. As we discussed in Chapter Two we are first introduced to this method of warfare in the Garden of Eden.

"Then the Lord God took the man and put him in the Garden of Eden to tend and keep it. And the Lord God commanded the man, saying, "Of every tree of the garden you may freely eat; but of the tree of the knowledge of good and evil you shall not eat, for in the day that you eat of it you shall surely die."(Genesis 2:15-17)

God was very specific in his directive to Adam and Eve concerning the tree of the knowledge of good and evil. They could have eaten of any tree in the garden, including the tree of Life, but instead they listened to the lies of the enemy rather than trusting in the words of God.

"Now the serpent was more cunning than any beast of the field which the Lord God had made. And he said to the woman, "Has God indeed said, 'You shall not eat of every tree of the garden?'" (Genesis 3:1)

We see this same tactic in the wilderness with Jesus. God has just declared Jesus to be His beloved Son.

"And suddenly a voice came from heaven, saying, "This is My beloved Son, in whom I am well pleased." (See Matthew 3:17)

And not two months later Satan is questioning what God said, *"If You are the Son of God..." (See Matthew 4:3)*

Satan will try and cast doubt upon the word that God has spoken to your heart. He will speak lies to you and try and make you question whether or not what God is saying is really true. He will use difficult circumstances to try and make you hesitate in your beliefs and question your faith. How did Jesus respond to this type of warfare? By *'taking up the sword of the Spirit, which is the Word of God.' (See Ephesians 6:17)*

"But Jesus answered and said, It is written, 'Man shall not live by bread alone, but by every word that proceeds from the mouth of God.'" (Matthew 4:4)

Jesus not only knew the Word of God, He knew how to effectively use it. The book of Proverbs tells us "*the heart of the righteous studies how to answer." (See Proverbs 15:28)* Paul tells us in his letter to Timothy that we are to study God's Word so that we may know how to present ourselves in any given circumstance.

"Study and be eager and do your utmost to present yourself to God approved (tested by trial), a workman who has no cause to be ashamed, correctly analyzing and accurately dividing [rightly handling and skillfully teaching] the Word of Truth." (2 Timothy 2:15 Amp)

The book of Proverbs advises us to lay up or store within us God's words making them readily available to us in our time of need. We cannot be ignorant of Satan's devices, lest he take advantage of us. If Satan cannot get us one way, he will try another way to trip us up and cause us defeat. Notice how he changed tactics when testing Jesus.

"Then the devil took Him up into the holy city, set Him on the pinnacle of the temple, and said to Him, "If you are the Son of God, throw Yourself down. For it is written:

'He shall give His angels charge over you,' and 'In their hands they shall bear you up, lest you dash your foot against a stone.'" (Matthew 4:5-6)

Once again Satan is trying to plant seeds of doubt and confusion as to the relationship Jesus holds with the Father. He questions his sonship challenging Jesus to test God at His Word. And this is where he changes tactics. Satan uses God's Word, knowingly misinterpreting the scriptures in the attempt to instill just enough doubt and unbelief to bring confusion to what God really said.

We cannot be ignorant of Satan's devices. We must know God's Word in order to rightfully discern that what is being said to us is truly God's Word. The book of Acts tells of those who:

"Received the word with all readiness, and searched the Scriptures daily to find out whether these things were so." (Acts 17:1b)

Let's take a look at how Jesus responded to this misuse of God's Word.

"Jesus said to him, On the other hand, it is written also, You shall not tempt, test thoroughly, or try exceedingly the Lord your God." (Matthew 4:7 Amp)

Satan knows the Word of God and he will use it against you in order to destroy your witness. It is imperative that we hide the Word of God in our hearts so we won't sin against Him. Jesus knew that what Satan was quoting was only partial truth. You will be quickly defeated if you try to come against the tactics of the enemy without having a clear understanding of God's Word.

It is not how much you know that's important, what matters is what you are doing with that knowledge. In other words, if you have studied God's Word and have memorized only one or two scriptures you have more power and authority in those few words, than someone who can quote the entire Bible but has no faith or understanding in what he is quoting. Look at what happened to the seven sons of Sceva.

"Then some of the itinerant Jewish exorcists took it upon themselves to call the name of the Lord Jesus over those who had evil spirits, saying 'We exorcise you by the Jesus whom Paul preaches.' Also there were seven sons of Sceva, a Jewish chief priest, who did so. And the evil spirit said, 'Jesus, I know, and Paul I know, but who are you?' Then the man in whom the evil spirit was leaped on them, overpowered them, and prevailed against them, so that they fled out of that house naked and wounded"(Acts 19:13-16)

Again, it is not the amount of scripture you know, it's what you've done with that amount that matters. God tells us in the book of Joshua that we are to meditate on His Word day and night.

"That you may observe to do according to all that is written in it. For then you will make your way prosperous, and then you will have good success." (Joshua 1:8)

Satan once again changes tactics in tempting Jesus. No longer does he question Jesus relationship with His Father, but now he tries to entice him with recognition and wealth, power and nobility.

"Again, the devil took Him up on an exceedingly high mountain, and showed Him all the kingdoms of the world and their glory. And he said to Him, "All these things I will give You, if You will fall down and worship me." Then Jesus said to him, "Away with you, Satan! For it is written, 'You shall worship the Lord your God, and Him only you shall serve. Then the devil left Him, and behold angels came and ministered to Him.'"(Matthew 4:8-11)

With every temptation, trial and test Jesus combated the enemy by thrusting the sword of the Spirit, which is the Word of God, into the very heart of his lies defeating him and forcing him to flee.

"Resist the devil [stand firm against him] and he will flee from you." (James 4:7 Amp)

Every time we speak God's Word, the two-edged sword of His Spirit strikes terror into the hearts of his toughest foe. In his letter to the Christians in Rome, Paul writes:

"The Word of God is near you, on your lips and in your heart; that is, the Word of faith that we preach." (Romans 10:8)

God promises us that He is faithful to watch over His Word. In fact, in the book of Jeremiah God says:

"I am alert and active, watching over My Word to perform it." (Jeremiah 1:12 Amp)

The prophet Isaiah tells us that as the word goes forth out of our mouth it will accomplish all that it was sent to do.

"It shall not return to Me void but it shall accomplish that which I please and purpose, and it shall prosper in the thing for which I sent it." (Isaiah 55:11)

The book of Hebrews tells us that the angels of God are His ministering servants. They hearken to His Word, and when we speak God's Word the angels go into action on our behalf.

It goes back to the scripture verses we previously studied in Corinthians:

"For the weapons of our warfare are not carnal but mighty in God for pulling down strongholds, casting down arguments and every high thing that exalts itself against the knowledge of God, bringing every thought into captivity to the obedience of Christ." (2 Corinthians 10:4-5)

When Satan speaks words of doubt and unbelief into our spirits, we need to cast down those arguments in the name of Jesus. We must bring every negative thought and feeling into captivity, stripping them of any hold they might have tried to take against us. How do we do that? We do this by simply speaking God's Word over those circumstances and situations in our lives.

What is it that you are facing today? What circumstances has Satan manipulated in order to cause you discomfort and discouragement? Has he brought sickness and disease against you or a loved one? You combat this attack of the devil the same way Jesus did in the wilderness. You take the Word of God, which is a two-edged sword, and you use it. For it is written:

"No weapon formed against you shall prosper."(Isaiah 54:17)

It is also written:

"What then shall we say to these things? If God is for us, who can be against us? He who did not spare His own Son, but delivered Him up for us all, how shall He not with Him also freely give us all things? Who shall bring a charge against God's elect?" (Romans 8:31-33)

What we must understand is the heart of God. He is for your health and prosperity. It was by the very stripes that Jesus bore on his flesh that we are healed.

"But He was wounded for our transgressions, He was bruised for our iniquities; the chastisement for our

peace was upon Him, and by His stripes we are healed." (Isaiah 53:5)

Have you lost hope? Have your hopes and dreams been damaged by the lies of Satan? Don't give up. Be strong in the power of His might. God says in His Word that He will give you the desires of your heart. Those hopes and dreams that have lain dormant for so long, God gave those to you. Take heart, God is the one who placed them there within your spirit, and He will be the one that will bring it to fruition.

"Do not fret because of evildoers, nor be envious of the workers of iniquity. For they shall soon be cut down like the grass, and wither as the green herb. Trust in the Lord, and do good; dwell in the land, and feed on His faithfulness. Delight yourself also in the Lord, and He shall give you the desires of your heart. Commit your way to the Lord, Trust also in Him, and He shall bring it to pass. He shall bring forth your righteousness as the light, and your justice as the noonday." (Psalms 37:1-6)

God's Word is active and it's alive. It's full of power and it's full of authority. Whatever your situation, find out what God says and then take Him at His Word.

"For the Word that God speaks is alive
and full of power making it active, operative,
energizing, and effective.
It is sharper than any two-edged sword,
penetrating to the dividing line of the breath of life and
spirit, and of joints and marrow,
exposing and sifting and analyzing and judging the very
thoughts and purposes of the heart.
And not a creature exists that is concealed from His sight,
but all things are open and exposed, naked and defenseless
to the eyes of Him with Whom we have to do. Inasmuch then
as we have a great High Priest

who has already ascended and passed through the heavens, Jesus the Son of God, let us hold fast our confession of faith in Him."
(Hebrews 4:12 -14)

Chapter Eight

Pray Without  *Ceasing*

"Praying always with all prayer and supplication in the Spirit, being watchful to this end with all perseverance and supplication for all the saints." (Ephesians 6:18)

Spiritual warfare is a reality for every Christian believer. It is not a *'ministry'* that only a select few are called to. It doesn't have to be scary or weird or something that's '*way out there*'. Spiritual warfare is simply having an understanding of who you are in Christ and walking in the fullness of that knowledge.

God has provided every believer with the spiritual armor necessary to successfully stand against the strategies and attacks of the enemy. Prayer is the essential ingredient, that activating force which releases the power to obtain the wisdom and understanding to effectively use this armor.

In Paul's letter to the Ephesians he emphasizes the necessity of prayer in a believers life. He not only instructs them to pray, but to pray constantly. Not only for themselves but also to be watchful and attentively persistent in praying for one another.

"Praying always with all prayer and supplication in the Spirit, being watchful to this end with all perseverance and supplication for all the saints." (Ephesians 6:18)

Though there are many forms of prayer, prayer is not a formula we use to get something from God. Webster's definition of the word '*pray*' is '*to make a request in a humble manner*; *to address God with adoration, confession, supplication, or thanksgiving.*'[xxii] Prayer is simply another form of communication. It is both listening to and speaking to God. We communicate with God for the sole purpose of establishing an intensely personal relationship with him. Through our prayer life we recognize God for who He is and we better understand who we are in Him.

As a soldier in God's army, we must understand that we are to be in constant communication with the One who knows all things, understands all things, and sees all things. Our Commander-in-Chief sees the whole battle, not only the little part that you and I are involved in. Through prayer, we are addressing the One who knows the outcome. A soldier that is adequately arrayed in armor but who has no direct line of communication with his Commander-in-Chief is in serious jeopardy. When the lines of communication are down, those on the battlefield are at great risk! With no instructions or clear directions as to what line of defense is to be taken, you will quickly lose ground and the enemy will gain ground in the battle.

We see this truth depicted in the Israelites first experience on the battlefield.

"Now Amalek came and fought with Israel in Rephidim. And Moses said to Joshua, "Choose us some men and go out, fight with Amalek. Tomorrow I will stand on the top of the hill with the rod of God in my hand." So Joshua did as Moses said to him, and fought with Amalek. And Moses, Aaron, and Hur went up to the top of the hill. And so it was, when Moses held up his hand, that Israel prevailed; and when he let down his hand, Amalek prevailed. But Moses' hands became heavy; so they took a stone and put it under him, and he sat on it. And Aaron and Hur supported his hands, one on one side, and the other on the other side;

and his hands were steady until the going down of the sun. So Joshua defeated Amalek and his people with the edge of the sword." (Exodus 17:8-13)

Amalek was a direct descendant of Esau, the twin brother of Jacob. Esau was the elder of the two and therefore was to receive the blessing of the firstborn. However he scorned his birthright and in a moment of weakness traded his rights as the oldest son in lieu of a hot cooked meal. He took that which was holy and used it for unholy purposes thus incurring a curse upon himself and his descendants. *(You can read his story in the 25th chapter of Genesis).*

The Amalekites were a nation that profaned, defiled and disdained the things of God just as their ancestor Esau. They neither feared nor respected Him. They were a type of the devil's hostility towards the seed of God (Christ), setting their hand against His throne and everything it represents.

Through God's direction Moses instructed Joshua to lead the Israelites in battle against the Amalekites. While Joshua and the Israelites were in the valley fighting the enemy, the Lord directed Moses to stand upon the hilltop with the rod of God extended in his hand. As long as the rod was lifted up over the battlefield, the Israelites prevailed. However, as soon as Moses lowered his arm, the enemy triumphed.

This rod not only represented God's presence, it also represented His power and authority. When Moses lifted the rod over the battlefield, God was declaring His presence not only to the Israelites but to their enemies as well. His power and authority was lifted above their circumstance ensuring the Israelites victory. However when Moses began tiring, his hands lowered causing the Israelites to lose sight of the symbolic representation of God's presence. When this happened they quickly began losing ground to the enemy.

As the battled waged on, Aaron and Hur recognized the weariness Moses was experiencing and came to his aid. Leading him to a rock so that he could sit and rest, they took his hands and together lifted up the rod of God. They supported him this way throughout the duration of the battle. Their obedience to God's direction enabled them to gain the victory in their lives.

Whether on the battlefield or not, we are all in this together and we must come to the aid of our brothers and sisters in need. However, in order to do this we must be aware of the situation around us and be attuned to the One giving direction. Had Moses not communicated with God, he would not have received the battle plan that led the Israelites to victory. Had Aaron and Hur not been aware of God's direction, they would not have understood the significance of lifting the rod of God high over the battlefield.

Prayer is an essential part of the armor of God. It is critical that we spend time with God in prayer. It is through prayer and quality time in God's word that we receive wisdom, discernment and direction in our lives. The defensive strategy that worked for yesterday's battle may not necessarily be the strategy that God wants us to use for today's battles.

What would have happened to Joshua and the Israelites if rather than seeking God's counsel concerning the city of Jericho, they had simply taken the rod of God and lifted it over the city? It worked before, why not again? Because this wasn't the plan God had for them. *(You can read this story in Joshua Chapter 6.)* Past victories are good because they remind us of the goodness of God. However yesterday's experiences were never meant to take the place of a fresh word from God.

In Paul's letter to the Ephesians he explains to them that they must be imitators of God. They must follow His example.

"Therefore be imitators of God [copy Him and follow His example], as well-beloved children [imitate their father]." (Ephesians 5:1 Amp)

God's example for us was and is Jesus Christ. He is the Son of Man and He is the Son of God, yet He still saw the necessity of spending time in prayer. How much more should we be seeking the heart of God in every area of our lives?

"And after He had dismissed the multitudes, He went up into the hills by Himself to pray, when it was evening, He was still there alone." (Matthew 14:23)

In the Gospel of Luke, Jesus spent the night in prayer seeking God's counsel as to whom He should choose to be his apostles.

"Now in those days it occurred that He went up into a mountain to pray, and spent the whole night in prayer to God. And when it was day, He summoned His disciples and selected from them twelve, whom he named apostles (special messengers)." (Luke 6:12-13 Amp)

Paul is instructing Christians everywhere that they were to be in a constant attitude of prayer. To be in touch with the Father, Son and Holy Spirit at all times throughout the day knowing that God hears every word and responds to every prayer. In the Gospel of John Jesus says that the Father always hears His prayers and is always listening for His voice.

"And Jesus lifted up His eyes and said, Father, I thank You that You have heard Me. Yes, I know You always hear and listen to Me." (John 11:41-42)

In the book of Romans God reveals Jesus as our intercessor. He goes to the Father on our behalf bringing us, and every need we have before Him knowing that God hears His prayers and answers every one.

"If God is for us, who can be against us? He who did not spare His own Son, but delivered Him up for us all, how shall He not with Him also freely give us all things? Who

shall bring a charge against God's elect? It is God who justifies. Who is he who condemns? It is Christ who died, and furthermore is also risen, who is even at the right hand of God, who also make intercession for us." (Romans 8:31-34)

In following Christ example we too must intercede on behalf of others understanding that God is attentive to our voice and hears our prayers as well. In the apostle Peter's first letter to the churches in the northern part of Asia Minor, he writes that God's eyes are upon the righteous and that He is attentive to their prayers.

"For the eyes of the Lord are on the righteous, and His ears are open [attentive] to their prayers;" (1 Peter 3:12 Amp)

The Lord speaks through the prophet Jeremiah telling us that when we call out to God, He will answer us and will show us great and mighty things.

"Call to Me and I will answer you and show you great and mighty things, fenced in and hidden, which you do not know (do not distinguish and recognize, have knowledge of and understand)." (Jeremiah 33:3 Amp)

When we come to the Father in prayer we receive the discernment and understanding needed to know how to go about reaching others for Jesus. Here again we must follow Christ's example in praying and interceding on behalf of others. In the book of Job, God promises to deliver the one for whom we intercede for.

"You will make your prayer to Him, and He will hear you, and you will pay your vows. You shall also decide and decree a thing, and it shall be established for you; and the light [of God's favor] shall shine upon your ways. When they make you low, you will say, There is a lifting up; and the

humble person He lifts up and saves, He will even deliver the one [for whom you intercede] who is not innocent; yes, he will be delivered through the cleanness of your hands." (Job 22:27-30 Amp)

We need to be watchful not only for ourselves but for those around us who are in need of prayer. In the Amplified translation this verse reads:

"Pray at all times (on every occasion, in every season) in the Spirit, with all [manner of] prayer and entreaty. To that end keep alert and watch with strong purpose and perseverance, interceding in behalf of all the saints." (Ephesians 6:18)

An example of interceding on someone else's behalf is the story of the paralytic found in the Gospel of Mark.

"And again He entered Capernaum after some days, and it was heard that He was in the house. Immediately many gathered together, so that there was no longer room to receive them, not even near the door. And He preached the word to them. Then they came to Him, bringing a paralytic who was carried by four men. And when they could not come near Him because of the crowd, they uncovered the roof where He was. So when they had broken through, they let down the bed on which the paralytic was lying." (Mark 2:1-4)

I can just imagine this scene. These men had a mission. They knew if they could get their friend to Jesus, He would heal him. But that was easier said then done. The crowd was so huge they couldn't push their way through even though they tried. Everyone wanted to hear what Jesus was saying, and no one was willing to give up their place, especially for someone they didn't know. Coming back wasn't an option. There was no way of knowing where Jesus would be tomorrow. And besides, Jesus Himself said that *"today was the day of salvation." (See Luke 19:9)* It had to be today.

I can just imagine the urgency in their hearts as they debated over what to do next. Standing there with their arms crossed, chin in hand, and eyes looking heavenward they see their answer. The rooftop. The only way to Jesus was up. These men were persistent. They didn't give up when they saw the crowds, or turn around in defeat when they realized they couldn't get to Jesus the conventional way.

Prayer will enable you to receive the wisdom and direction you need to overcome every obstacle standing in your way. These men needed to get their friend to Jesus, and God showed them how.

"And when they could not get him to a place in front of Jesus because of the throng, they dug through the roof above Him; and when they had scooped out an opening, they let down the [thickly padded] quilt or mat upon which the paralyzed man lay." (Mark 2:4 Amp)

The preparation necessary to get their friend to Jesus was a very well thought out process. First of all, these men would have to see to it that their friend was securely fastened to keep him safe as they lowered him through the roof. Next they would need to check their footing making sure that wherever they stepped it would be a solid enough foundation to hold them. If they stumbled, the likelihood of this man falling was even greater. They also had to exude confidence to their friend that no matter what, they weren't going to let him down – figuratively or literally. Even a few inches would be a long way to fall when you have no way to brace yourself and nothing to stop the impact.

The strength of character these men possessed must have been incredible. It was a strength that would carry them through no matter what the obstacle. A strength that instilled perseverance and tenacity into the very core of their being, breeding a determination that could not be deterred. Nothing was going to stop them or keep them from accomplishing this goal. They would bring their precious friend to Jesus. Theirs was a faith that you could see and feel, and it touched the heart of God.

"And when Jesus saw their faith [their confidence in God through Him], He said to the paralyzed man, Son, your sins are forgiven [you] and put away [that is, the penalty is remitted, the sense of guilt removed, and you are made upright and in right standing with God]." (Mark 2:5 Amp)

This is a picture of what happens in the spirit realm when we intercede for someone. It is simply taking that one in need to Jesus. No matter what the cost, we will not stop or be deterred until they are at the feet of Jesus receiving all that He has for them. This is what Paul meant when he said to watch out for those in need, to be persistent in your prayers for them. Not giving up until they've received the victory God has promised them.

During Paul's incarceration he had opportunity to witness the Roman soldiers practicing their battle formations and various strategic moves. One such formation the Roman soldiers would use during battle would be to stand side by side with their shields in front of them. The soldiers standing behind would then raise their shields covering the tops of the heads of the soldiers in front. This made the advancing group of Romans an impregnable wall that couldn't be broken without many casualties. At the Centurion's command, the front lines would move to the back while the others moved forward. This would keep the front line soldiers from wearying in the battle and less vulnerable to attack. Communication was vital to implementing a successful assault against the enemy.

Prayer is an integral part of the armor of God. Without it, our armor is incomplete and lacking. It is imperative that we understand that we can actually strengthen the effectiveness of not only our armor, but that of our Christian brothers and sisters as we pray. It is through prayer that God grants us the necessary power to operate in the wisdom and discernment of God. It is a highly effective weapon that not only unites the body of Christ, but it also enables us to advance against the enemy.

There will be times in our lives where we find ourselves weary and tired. Like Moses we have lifted God's Word over our present circumstances but our arms have become heavy with the weight of the battle. At times like these we need the *'Aarons and Hurs'* in our lives to stand along side us, praying and interceding on our behalf.

At other times, we find ourselves in the role of Aaron and Hur: We are the ones coming along side the *Moses'* in our lives gently leading and guiding them to rest upon the Rock of Salvation, Jesus Christ. Together we will lift our voices in prayer supporting them this way throughout the duration of the battle. For we are an army united. Standing side by side with shields lifted high, together we raise our voices in prayer as we continue marching forward in absolute confidence and victory.

"These "soldiers" charge like infantry; they scale the walls like picked and trained commandos. Straight forward they march, never breaking ranks. They never crowd each other. Each is right in place. No weapon can stop them. The Lord leads them with a shout. This is His mighty army and they follow His orders."
(Joel 2:7-8; & 11 TLB)

Chapter Nine

Armed In  *Deity*

"But clothe yourselves with the Lord Jesus Christ…" (Romans 13:14a)

As soldiers in God's army we have been called, anointed and equipped with the spiritual armor that empowers us to stand against the devil with all his strategies and deceit. Through Paul's letter to the Ephesians we have learned the significance of each piece and the vital role it plays in our walking and living a victorious life in Christ. Paul described this armor to us by comparing it to the physical armor of a Roman soldier. We've learned that a full suite of armor consists of a belt, breastplate, shoes, shield, helmet and sword. He also explained the soldier's need for a direct line of communication with those in authority.

Now let's take a look at God's armor without these physical comparisons. His armor consists of truth, righteousness, peace, faith, salvation, the word of God and prayer. When God instructed us to put on His armor, He was in essence commanding us to clothe ourselves with Himself.

In his letter to the Romans the apostle Paul says:

"But put on the Lord Jesus Christ and make no provision for the flesh, to fulfill its lust." (Romans 13:14)

The definition of the phrase *'put on'* means to *'clothe oneself; to sink into'.*[xxiii]

When Paul was instructing the Ephesians to put on the armor of God, piece by piece, he was telling them to put on the Lord Jesus Christ. We are to clothe ourselves with truth. In the Gospel of John, Pontius Pilate ask Jesus the question, "What is truth?"*(See John 18:38)* Prior to this encounter Jesus was asked a similar question by one of his disciples.

"Lord, we do not know where you are going, and how can we know the way?"(John 14:5)

Jesus responded by saying:

"I am the way, the truth, and the life. No one comes to the Father except through me." (John 14:6)

Jesus Christ is truth and we are to clothe or arm ourselves with this truth every moment of every day.

Scripture tells us that God's own righteousness sustained Him when he looked upon the devastation sin brought upon His creation. The prophet Isaiah is quoted as saying:

"His own arm brought Him victory, and His own righteousness sustained Him. For the Lord put on righteousness as a breastplate." (Isaiah 59:16b Amp)

Here again the definition for the phrase *'put on'* means to *clothe oneself; to sink into'.*[xxiv]

In Paul's first letter to the Christians in Corinth he explains to them that it is through God that we have our life in Christ. Jesus stated this truth in the Gospel of John when he said:

"No one is able to come to Me unless the Father who sent Me attracts and draws him and gives him the desire to come to Me". (John 6:44 Amp)

Paul reiterates this truth in his letter saying that not only is it because of God that we are in Christ Jesus, but it was God who made Jesus our righteousness.

"But it is from Him that you have your life in Christ Jesus, whom God made our Wisdom from God, our Righteousness, our Consecration and our Redemption." (1 Corinthians 1:30)

Jesus is our righteousness and God is commanding us to clothe ourselves or arm ourselves with this righteousness. Once again we find ourselves putting on the Lord Jesus Christ so that we become the righteousness of God in Him.

"For He made Him who knew no sin to be sin for us, that we might become the righteousness of God in Him." (2 Corinthians 5:21)

In his letter to the Ephesians Paul is instructing Christians to:

"Put on the new man which was created according to God, in true righteousness and holiness." (Ephesians 4:24)

In the Amplified translation this verse reads:

"And put on the new nature (the regenerate self) created in God's image, [Godlike] in true righteousness and holiness."(Ephesians 4:24 Amp)

This new nature that we are putting on or clothing ourselves in is the nature of God. We are taking on His attributes and His characteristics enabling us to represent

Him to this world with excellence. In the book of Colossians we are instructed to clothe ourselves as God's chosen representatives, putting on behavior typical of Jesus Christ.

"Therefore, as the elect of God holy and beloved, put on tender mercies, kindness, humility, meekness, longsuffering; bearing with one another, and forgiving one another, if anyone has a complaint against another, even as Christ forgave you, so you also must do. But above all these things, put on love, which is the bond of perfection." (Colossians 3:12-14)

Not only do we clothe our self with the characteristics of God but we are to *'put on'* love. According to 1st John 4:8 "*God is love*". So here again we see God instructing us to clothe ourselves with Himself.

The writer of the book of Hebrews refers to Jesus as being the King of Righteousness and the King of Peace.

"*...Jesus, having become High Priest forever according to the order of Melchizedek. For this Melchizedek, king of Salem, priest of the Most High God, who met Abraham returning from the slaughter of the kings and blessed him, to whom also Abraham gave a tenth part of all, first being translated "king of righteousness", and then also king of Salem, meaning "king of peace," without father, without mother, without genealogy, having neither beginning of days nor end of life, but made like the Son of God, remains a priest continually." (Hebrews 6:20b; 7:1-3)*

The next piece of armor God is instructing us to arm ourselves with is peace. Once again we are to put on the Lord Jesus Christ who is our peace.

Paul introduces this truth to the Ephesians when he says:

"For He Himself is our peace". (Ephesians 2:14)

The prophet Isaiah also declared that Jesus was the Prince of Peace.

"For unto us a Child is born, unto us a Son is given' and the government will be upon His shoulder. And His name will be called Wonderful, Counselor, Mighty God, Everlasting Father, Prince of Peace." (Isaiah 9:6 Amp)

In his letter to the Colossians Paul instructs Christians to let the peace of God, which is Jesus, rule their hearts. When Jesus is ruling your heart, your emotions and feelings are not. In fact, when you allow the peace of God to rule and reign in your heart your emotions and feelings subject themselves to His authority.

The next part of Jesus character that God wants us to clothe ourselves in is that of faith. In Chapter Five we learned that Jesus bears the name *'Faithful'* in the book of Revelation.

"Now I saw heaven opened, and behold, a white horse. And He who sat on him was called Faithful and True, and in righteousness He judges and makes war." (Revelation 19:11)

When we put faith on we are clothing ourselves with the One who is faithful and true. This covering of faith motivates and prompts us to fulfill God's divine purpose for our lives deflecting and extinguishing every fiery dart. Clothing ourselves in the faith of the Son of God brings Him great pleasure, for without faith it is impossible to please God.

"But without faith it is impossible to please Him, for he who comes to God must believe that He is, and that He is a rewarder of those who diligently seek Him." (Hebrews 11:6)

The next piece of God's armor that Paul introduces us to is that of salvation. In the book of Isaiah we've learned that salvation is a garment that God has graciously clothed us in. *(See Isaiah 61:10)* we've also learned through the prophet Zechariah how God removed the filthy rags of sin in exchange for these garments. *(See Zechariah 3:4)*

In the book of Ephesians Jesus is referred to as being the head of the church, which is also known as the body of Christ. In this same passage it also refers to the husband being the head or the covering for his wife. *(See Ephesians 5:23)* Jesus is our covering of protection and defense. He is our Savior. In fact, His very name means "*Jehovah is salvation*".[xxv] Remember the words of Paul in Ephesians, how he compares salvation to that of a helmet covering the head. Jesus is our head. He is our covering. When we put on salvation, here again we are clothing ourselves or immersing ourselves into the Lord Jesus Christ.

Paul continues to instruct Christians everywhere to arm themselves with God's Word. In the Gospel of John Jesus is called the Word of God.

"In the beginning was the Word, and the Word was with God, and the Word was God. And the Word became flesh and dwelt among us, and we beheld His glory, the glory as of the only begotten of the Father, full of grace and truth." (John 1:1&14)

The apostle John reiterates this truth in the book of Revelation when he says:

"*He is dressed in a robe dyed by dipping in blood, and the title by which He is called is The Word of God.*" (Revelation 19:13 Amp)

He also states that:

"From His mouth goes forth a sharp sword." (Revelation 19:15 Amp)

Jesus Christ is the Word of God. It is His Word that we speak, and His Word that we stand upon. Paul instructs Christians to take up the helmet of salvation and the sword of the Spirit, which is the Word of God. Referring back to Chapter Six, we are reminded that the phrase, '*take up*' means '*to be granted access to*'. We have been granted access to the salvation of God and the Word of God through Jesus Christ Himself.

The last piece of armor mentioned is that of prayer. We are to clothe ourselves in prayer as well, but it's more than just that. We must understand that Jesus is not only the personification of the aforementioned armor; He is also our prayer warrior. In Paul's letter to the Romans he says:

"It is Christ who died, and furthermore is also risen, who is even at the right hand of God, who also makes intercession for us." (Romans 8:34)

The writer of Hebrews also states:

"Therefore He is able also to save to the uttermost (completely, perfectly, finally and for all time and eternity) those who come to God through Him, since He is always living to make petition to God and intercede with Him and intervene for them." (Hebrews 7:23 Amp)

God has used the writings of Paul to speak to Christians everywhere about the importance of understanding spiritual warfare and how vital it is to be completely armed. There was a sense of urgency in Paul's words to the Romans when he wrote:

"You know what a critical hour this is, how it is high time now for you to wake up out of your sleep (rouse to reality). For salvation is nearer to us now than when we first believed. The night is far gone and the day is almost here. Let us then drop (fling away) the works and deeds of

darkness and put on the full armor of light." (Romans 13:11-12 Amp)

Paul is emphasizing the importance of putting on the full armor, only this time he refers to it as the armor of light. Here again, the phrase *'putting on'* simply means *'to clothe yourself'*. But what does he mean by *'armor of light'*? To fully understand the significance of what Paul is trying to convey here, we must go back to the beginning.

As we discussed in Chapter Two Adam and Eve's act of disobedience caused a separation from God that they had never experienced before. Prior to their fallen state they were surrounded by God's presence. Although they were naked there was no shame for the light of God's glory was their covering. When Adam and Eve chose to disobey God's command, their sin separated them from His presence. His glory departed and they found themselves naked and exposed in their sin. Instead of longing for His presence they hid from Him in fear and humiliation.

"So when the woman saw that the tree was good for food, that it was pleasant to the eyes, and a tree desirable to make one wise, she took of its fruit and ate. She also gave to her husband with her, and he ate. Then the eyes of both of them were opened, and they knew that they were naked; and they sewed fig leaves together and made themselves coverings. And they heard the sound of the Lord God walking in the garden in the cool of the day, and Adam and his wife hid themselves from the presence of the Lord God..." (Genesis 3:6-8 Amp)

When Adam and Eve recognized their nakedness they tried sewing fig leaves together in order to make a covering for themselves. The definition of the word *'coverings'* according to the Strong's Concordance is, *'armor'*.[xxvi] The consequence of Adam and Eve's disobedience wasn't just physical death. Their sin also caused a separation not only from God's presence but from His covering as well.

In his letter to the Christians in Rome, Paul explains that God has once again provided a means for them to be covered with the light of His presence.

"Let us then drop (fling away) the works and deeds of darkness and put on the full armor of light" (Romans 13:12)

In the Gospel of John it is written:

"In Him was life, and the life was the light of men." (John 1:4)

Jesus reiterated this truth when he said:

"I am the light of the world. He who follows Me shall not walk in darkness, but have the light of life." (John 8:12)

Jesus Christ is the armor or covering God has instructed us to clothe ourselves in. We are to put on the Lord Jesus Christ and all His attributes so that we may successfully stand against the devil and all his cohorts. Our spiritual clothing is to be layered with truth, righteousness, peace, faith, salvation, the Word of God and prayer. We have been created in the likeness and image of God and therefore go from glory to glory armed in His deity. As an army chosen, anointed and equipped by God, we are more than conquerors having gained a surpassing victory through the death and resurrection power of the Lord Jesus Christ. **ARMED AND VICTORIOUS** we stand!

"Therefore take up the whole armor of God,
that you may be able to withstand in the evil day,
and having done all to stand,
Stand therefore..."
(Ephesians 6:13-14a)

Study Guide - Introduction

Armed & Victorious

Throughout scripture we see a picture of mankind being dominated and held captive by sin's ugly clutches.

a. In Romans 3:10-18 how does Paul describe mankind?

____

____

____

b. According to Isaiah 59:1-5 what caused our separation from God?

____

____

____

The book of Isaiah tells us that there was no one who could pay the price for our sin. God searched for someone to intercede on behalf of His creation, but there was no one.

a. According to Isaiah 59:16-17, who came to our rescue?

____

____

____

b. How did God demonstrate His love for us?

____

____

____

Jesus came and through the cross He conquered Satan, totally disarming him and all his demons, stripping them of all power and authority over those who put their trust in Jesus Christ as Lord and Savior.

a. In Zechariah 3:2-4 what does God have removed from off of us?

____

____

____

b. What does He put on us in its place?

____

____

____

c. How does Isaiah 61:10 describe this new wardrobe?

____

____

____

All power and authority has been given to Jesus who in turn has given us that same power and authority in His name.

a. How do we receive this power and authority?

____

____

____

b. According to Luke 10:19, what does this power and authority enable us to do?

____

____

____

God armed Himself to do battle with the enemy, and He has passed down His armor to us.

a. How was this armor passed down to us?

____

____

____

b. Why did God give us His armor?

____

____

____

The battle has been fought and the enemy has been conquered. This glorious victory has been handed over to you and I.

a. Through the death and resurrection of Jesus Christ what have you and I become?

____

____

____

b. What have we gained through the death and resurrection of Jesus Christ?

____

____

____

Study Guide – Chapter One

A Call To Arms

The apostle Paul is writing this letter to the Christians in Ephesus from the confines of a prison cell in Rome.

a. From his area of confinement what is Paul able to observe?

____

____

____

b. What comparison was Paul able to make?

____

____

____

As Paul concludes this letter he reminds them to draw their strength from God and to rely upon His power and might.

a. When did they receive this ruling power?

____

____

____

b. What does this ruling power bring to our lives?

____

____

____

Paul explains to the fellow believers in Ephesus that our battle is not with one another. We are not wrestling with each other, but our battle is against Satan and all his cohorts.

a. According to 2 Corinthians 10:3-4 what are we not suppose to do?

____

____

____

b. What kind of weapons has God provided us with?

____

____

____

For this reason Paul tells us that we must take up the complete armor of God. In order to successfully stand up against the enemy we must take up every piece of armor.

a. What does the belt of truth represent?

____

____

____

b. What does the breastplate of righteousness represent?

____

____

____

c. What does covering our feet with the preparation of the Gospel of peace mean?

____

____

____

d. What does taking up the shield of faith mean?

____

____

____

e. What does the helmet of salvation cover?

____

____

____

f. What is the sword of the spirit?

____

____

____

g. How do we keep a direct line of communication open?

____

____

____

It is imperative we understand that Paul is trying to convey to us that there is a vast difference between wrestling and standing.

a. According to Webster's Dictionary, how is the word '*wrestle*' defined?

____

____

____

b. What is the definition of '*stand*'?

____

____

____

c. If we are wrestling what two pieces of armor must we lay down?

____

____

____

d. What kind of military stance does God want us to take?

____

____

____

Once Paul explains about putting on the full armor of God and describes the pieces of that armor, he never mentions wrestling again.

a. Does this mean that we will never have difficulties, trials or temptations again?

____

____

____

b. As soldiers we are marching towards something and from something. What are these things?

____

____

____

c. According to John 16:33 what will we have?

____

____

____

d. Why should we be of good cheer?

____

____

____

e. Why did God provide us with heavenly armor?

____

____

____

f. If we resist the devil what will happen?

____

____

____

Nehemiah understood the principle of resisting the enemy. As part of their defense against the enemy he told the workers that no matter where they were positioned on the wall, when they heard the trumpet blast they were to converge to that area with their swords drawn ready to come to the assistance of their brother in need.

a. According to Nehemiah 4:17-20 what did the soldiers hold in their hands?

____

____

____

b. Who was to fight on their behalf?

____

____

____

c. When the enemy heard that their plot had been exposed what did they do?

____

____

____

d. How are you and I like Nehemiah?

____

____

____

As in the days of Nehemiah, we too have an enemy who is enraged over the progress we are making. The enemy plots against us with the intention of causing injury, confusion and failure.

a. According to John 10:10 what does Jesus call the devil?

____

____

____

b. How must we deal with the devil?

____

____

____

c. What does it mean to be given a '*Call to Arms*'?

____

____

____

Study Guide – Chapter Two

The Belt of Truth

God has provided you and I with the weapons that will protect and defend the victorious life He has granted us. Even though our enemy is not of flesh and blood, he is very real.

a. What is the first piece of armor that we are to put on?

____

____

____

b. What must our life be founded upon?

____

____

____

c. What is a direct threat against the enemy of God?

____

____

____

From the beginning of time Satan has tried to steal the truth from the heart of God's people.

a. How does Satan manipulate God's Word?

____

____

____

b. How does he cast doubt in the hearts and minds of people?

___

___

___

c. According to Genesis 3:1-4 how did Satan question God's authority?

___

___

___

d. What did Eve choose over God's word?

___

___

___

Satan came with his trickery and deceit blinding the eyes of Adam and Eve to the truth of God's word.

a. What were the consequences of Adam and Eve's sin?

___

___

___

b. What did their sin cause them to do?

___

___

___

c. After being banished from the Garden of Eden why did they have hope in their hearts?

___

___

___

It is imperative that we know the truth, and are secure in that truth. We must be secure in our knowledge of who Jesus is and what He did.

a. What will free us from the dominion of sin?

b. What will truth do for us?

The Roman soldiers guarding Paul understood the importance of the leather belt that made up part of their armor.

a. What was the sole purpose of the leather belt?

b. How does our *'spiritual belt'* compare to the soldiers belt?

c. What does the truth of the Gospel of Jesus Christ free us from?

Study Guide – Chapter Three

The Breastplate of Righteousness

In preparation for facing the enemy, a Roman soldier would fasten his leather belt to his waist. Once this was secure, the soldier would then put on the breastplate attaching it to his belt. Paul is instructing us to put on God's righteousness the same way a soldier puts on his breastplate.

a. How does righteousness protect us?

____

____

____

b. Whose righteousness are we putting on?

____

____

____

c. What is our righteousness like in comparison to God's?

____

____

____

d. How do we receive God's righteousness?

____

____

____

As we call upon the name of the Lord Jesus, God removes the sin-covered garments we were clothed in and covers us with His garments of salvation.

a. Why did Jesus become sin for us?

____

____

____

b. What is the definition of *'righteousness'* according to Webster's Dictionary?

____

____

____

c. What does the word *'defend'* mean?

____

____

____

d. How is the word *'encroachment'* defined?

____

____

____

e. How have we been freed from the guilt and penalty of sin?

____

____

____

Paul tells us to put on God's complete armor in order to successfully stand against the strategies and deceits of the devil. Satan will try to stealthily enter our domain by taking gradual steps, so as to not be noticed.

a. What is Satan trying to steal, kill and destroy?

____

____

____

b. How does God's righteousness protect and defend us?

____

____

____

c. How does God's righteousness put us in right standing with Him?

____

____

____

d. What does God's righteousness enable us to possess?

____

____

____

Jesus is Truth, and our righteousness is based upon that truth. It is the revelation that everything I have belongs to Jesus, everything I am is because of Him, and everything I do is through His power and authority.

a. According to Zechariah 4:6 if it isn't by our might and strength then by whose?

____

____

____

b. Who lives in and through us?

____

____

____

c. Why is it that guilt and condemnation no longer have a hold on us?

____

____

____

Paul is saying that we are to put off the old man or the old nature. The old ways of doing things and the old ways of responding are no longer acceptable.

a. What are we replacing our old nature with?

____

____

____

b. Who is this righteousness made available to?

____

____

____

c. In the parable of the wedding feast, what did the guest refuse?

____

____

____

d. What gifts are we forfeiting when we deny the garments of the King?

____

____

____

e. What does God's righteousness empower us to do?

____

____

____

Study Guide – Chapter Four

The Shoes of the Gospel of Peace

As a prisoner of the Roman guard, Paul could understand the importance of balance and positioning in the Christian's life. He could also appreciate the significance of being prepared and ready.

a. According to Ephesians 6:14 Paul is instructing us to cover our feet in preparation for what?

____

____

____

b. What does God's peace produce in our lives?

____

____

____

c. How is the word *'peace'* defined according to the Amplified Version of Philippians 4:7?

____

____

____

d. According to Isaiah 32:17 peace is the effect of what?

____

____

____

Having our feet shod with the preparedness of the gospel of peace will enable us to walk and lead a life worthy of the divine calling to which you and I have been called.

a. In Isaiah 40:31 what does the prophet declare?

____

____

____

b. According to Proverbs 4:12 what promise is God giving to us?

____

____

____

c. According to Habakkuk 3:17 our feet are compared to hinds feet. Why?

____

____

____

d. What does '*having our feet shod*' mean?

____

____

____

It was Paul's intention to help Christians understand that in the same manner that a Roman soldier used his footwear to trample the enemy, the gospel of peace enables us to trample upon our enemies.

a. What did Jesus tell the disciples they had the power to do in Luke 10:19?

____

____

____

b. How can we intimidate the enemy?

Satan knows that balance and positioning are important aspects to a Christian's life. Therefore he will do whatever it takes to throw us off center.

a. How will Satan try to throw us off center?

b. What types of weapons will he use against us?

c. In what ways might he attack you?

d. How can we combat these attacks?

e. According to 2 Corinthians 10:4-5 what was Paul's advice?

In Paul's letter to the Christians in Philippi, he explains to them that God's peace will keep their heart.

a. What does the word *'keep'* mean when translated from the Greek language?

____

____

____

b. How does God's peace compare to that of the Roman garrison guarding the city of Philippi?

____

____

____

Having our *'feet shod'* with the gospel of peace implies standing and walking in God's power and authority. It speaks of preparation and possession. It also represents sonship.

a. In the parable of the prodigal son, what did the son leave in search of?

____

____

____

b. How did the son go from riches to rags in such a short time?

____

____

____

c. What finally convinced the son to return to his father's home?

____

____

____

d. When the son came near to his home who met him?

e. What was the response of the father upon seeing this son?

This story ended differently than the younger son anticipated.

a. Instead of condemnation and rejection what did the younger son receive?

b. What did he receive instead of a death sentence for dishonoring his father?

c. How did his father shower him with favor?

d. In those days, what did it mean to go *'barefoot'*?

e. What did the robe upon his back and the shoes upon his feet represent?

____

____

____

God prepares and arms us with the ability to advance against the enemy.

a. According to Romans 16:20 what does the God of peace do to Satan?

____

____

____

b. What are we to be committed to?

____

____

____

c. We have been ____________, ______________, and _______________ and now we must go in the power and the authority given to us by God Himself.

Study Guide – Chapter Five

The Shield of Faith

a. What is the significance of the soldier's belt? Breastplate? Shoes?

____

____

____

b. The Roman soldier's shield was designed to protect him from what?

____

____

____

During this time in history, it was common practice to wrap the tips of arrows in linen and then soak them in pitch. The tip of the arrow was then ignited and shot at the enemy.

a. What was the most reliable protection against these flaming missiles?

____

____

____

b. With what did the Roman soldiers anoint their shields?

____

____

____

c. What kinds of fiery darts does Satan throw at us?

____

____

____

In his letter to the Ephesians, Paul says that it is imperative that we receive God's protective covering, taking hold of it with a firm grip and lift it up above all else.

a. What is this protective covering we are to lift up?

____

____

____

b. We've put on the belt of truth acknowledging what?

____

____

____

c. The breastplate of righteousness exchanges our _______________ for Christ's _________________.

d. With every step the shoes of the gospel of peace enable us to bring ____________ and ____________________ to those around us.

e. What have you and I received a measure of?

____

____

____

Above all else we are to lift up the shield of faith, the protective covering of God's faithfulness that deflects and extinguishes every fiery dart the enemy hurls our way.

a. According to Psalms 91, how does David describe the protective covering of God?

____

____

____

b. According to Revelation 19:1 what is God called?

____

____

____

c. How is the word *'faithful'* defined according to the Webster's Dictionary?

____

____

____

d. According to 2 Timothy 2:13 how does God respond when we are faithless?

____

____

____

Moses and the children of Israel knew firsthand what it was like to experience God's faithful covering.

a. When the Israelites cried out to God because of their bondage, what was His response?

____

____

____

b. According to Exodus 14:13-14 who was going to fight this battle for the Israelites?

____

____

____

c. How did God's faithfulness protect the Israelites at the Red Sea?

____

____

____

d. On what side does God's faithfulness cover us?

____

____

____

God speaks to us through the prophet Isaiah telling us that it is His righteousness that shall go before us, and His glory, which shall be our rear guard.

a. What does the phrase *'rear guard'* mean?

____

____

____

b. God's ____________ within us is an active force that motivates, urges and prompts us to fulfill God's divine purpose for our lives.

c. According to 2 Peter 1:5-7 what happens when we exercise our faith?

____

____

____

d. What are we to station in front of all the other parts of armor?

____

____

____

e. The belt of truth cannot function apart from what?

____

____

____

f. The breastplate of righteousness cannot operate apart from what?

____

____

____

g. The sandals of peace cannot effectively work aside from what?

____

____

____

h. When we recognize Satan's lies how do we take up the shield of faith?

____

____

____

i. When the fiery darts of doubt and unbelief are hurled at us how do we extinguish them?

____

____

____

Study Guide – Chapter Six

The Helmet of Salvation

In battle, the two most vulnerable areas of attack are the heart and the head. These were the targets of the enemy. If a soldier is wounded in either of these places the end result was most likely death. For this reason, the helmet was as crucial a part of the soldier's armor as the breastplate.

a. What was the most important factor in determining a soldier's victory or defeat?

____

____

____

b. If a soldier went into battle unprepared and his head exposed, how would this diminish his fighting ability?

____

____

____

c. Why must we as Christians be prepared with our minds focused and our thoughts lining up with God's word?

____

____

____

d. How can Satan gain victory in our lives?

____

____

____

God has provided us with His helmet of salvation. This is our protective covering of healing, soundness and wholeness that we may successfully stand against the wiles, strategies and deceitfulness of the enemy.

a. What have we been granted access to through the redemptive sacrifice of Jesus Christ?

____

____

____

b. What does the phrase *'putting on'* mean?

____

____

____

c. The helmet of salvation protects us from a ______________ mind, a ______________ mind, a ______________ mind and a ______________ mind.

d. What is the difference between the modern day usage of the word 'hope' and the biblical usage of this word?

____

____

____

e. According to Hebrews 6:19 how is God's hope described?

____

____

____

The helmet of salvation enables the believer to maintain total confidence of victory, no matter how long the battle may seem to last. It empowers us to see beyond where we are to the bigger picture – the fulfillment of God's promises.

a. What does the word *'repent'* mean according to the Amplified Bible?

____

____

____

b. Our Christian life grows as our mind is ________ and __________.

God's desire is for us to grow in the grace and knowledge of the Lord Jesus Christ, walking according to His Spirit and not according to our flesh.

a. According to Romans 8:1 those who are in Christ Jesus walk according to the ________.

b. In order for us to live according to God's Spirit, what must we do?

____

____

____

c. According to Philippians 4:8 what things are we to think upon?

____

____

____

Though the battle belongs to the Lord, we are still in a battle. This is why God provided us with the spiritual weaponry to defeat the enemy in our lives.

a. How has the enemy been declared powerless in our lives?

b. Since the battle belongs to the Lord, what is our responsibility?

c. According to 2 Thessalonians 2:2 what does it mean to be *'shaken'*?

d. What will cause us to be shaken in our stance against the enemy?

e. What is the prayer of King David in Psalms 19:4?

f. According to 2 Corinthians 10:3-5 how do we combat thoughts contrary to God's word?

g. What does the phrase *'casting down'* mean?

____

____

____

h. What does the word *'imaginations'* mean?

____

____

____

Paul is instructing us to cast down or demolish any word, thought, or purpose that would elevate itself over God's rightful place in our lives.

a. According to 1 Peter 4:1 how do we guard our thought life?

____

____

____

b. How do we arm ourselves with the mind of Christ?

____

____

____

Faith is of the heart, whereas hope is of the mind. The helmet of salvation represents the protective covering for the mind of the saved person.

a. How is our mind both transformed and renewed?

____

____

____

b. When does our mind become obedient to Christ?

____

____

____

c. What does the helmet of salvation enable us to do?

____

____

____

As our minds remain steadfast we are kept in peace, understanding that this salvation represents all that Christ has done for us.

Study Guide – Chapter Seven

The Sword of the Spirit

In his letter to the Ephesians, Paul is likening the Word of God that the Spirit wields to that of the double-edged Machiara Sword used by the Romans. It was both highly effective and devastating to its enemy.

a. According to Hebrews 4:12 the Word that God speaks is both _________ and full of ___________.

b. According to this verse, what does the Word of God do?

____

____

____

c. What weapon did Jesus use against the devil when tested and tried in the wilderness?

____

____

____

d. What is one of enemy's greatest tactics of defense?

____

____

____

e. When was the method of warfare first introduced?

___

___

___

God was very specific in his directive to Adam and Eve concerning the tree of the knowledge of good and evil.

a. How did Satan instill doubt and confusion in the heart of Eve?

___

___

___

b. When Satan tried this tactic on Jesus how did Jesus respond?

___

___

___

c. According to 2 Timothy 2:15 why must we study God's word?

___

___

___

We cannot be ignorant of Satan's devices, lest he take advantage of us. If Satan cannot get us one way, he will try another way to trip us up to bring defeat.

a. How did Satan change tactics when tempting Jesus?

___

___

___

b. What question does Satan ask Jesus in the hope of instilling doubt?

____

____

____

c. How does Jesus respond to this misuse of God's word?

____

____

____

Satan knows the Word of God and he will use it against you in order to destroy your witness.

a. Why should we hide God's word in our hearts?

____

____

____

b. How can we know if scripture is being misquoted or misrepresented?

____

____

____

c. According to Acts 19:13-16, what happens when faith and understanding is not mixed with knowledge?

____

____

____

d. According to Joshua 1:8, why should we meditate upon God's word?

____

____

____

With every temptation, trial and test Jesus combated the enemy by thrusting the sword of the Spirit, which is the Word of God, into the very heart of his lies defeating him and forcing him to flee.

a. What will cause Satan to flee from us?

____

____

____

b. What happens when we use the double-edged sword of God's word?

____

____

____

c. What is God's promise to us in Jeremiah 1:12?

____

____

____

d. What is God's promise to us in Isaiah 55:11?

____

____

____

e. What kinds of weapons has God given us?

____

____

____

f. According to 2 Corinthians 10:3-4 what will these weapons do?

____

____

____

g. How do we cast down evil imaginations?

____

____

____

We must understand the heart of God. He is for us and not against us. His Word is active and alive, full of power and authority. Whatever your situation, find out what God says and then take Him at His Word.

Study Guide – Chapter Eight

Pray Without Ceasing

God provided every believer with the spiritual armor necessary to successfully stand against the strategies and attacks of the enemy.

a. What is spiritual warfare?

____

____

____

b. Who is called to this ministry?

____

____

____

c. What is essential to release the power to obtain the wisdom and understanding to effectively use this armor?

____

____

____

In Paul's letter to the Ephesians he emphasizes the necessity of prayer in a believer's life.

a. According to Ephesians 6:18 when are we to pray?

___

___

___

b. Who are we to pray for?

___

___

___

c. What is the definition of the word *'pray'*?

___

___

___

d. Is there a formula we can use to get our prayers answered?

___

___

___

e. Why do we communicate with God?

___

___

___

f. What does a consistent prayer life enable us to do?

___

___

___

As a soldier in God's army, we must understand that we are to be in constant communication with the One who knows all things, understands all things, and sees all things. Our Commander-in-Chief sees the entire battle and He knows where we are at all times.

a. What happens if a soldier has no communication with those in authority?

____

____

____

b. When the lines of communication are down, what happens on the battlefield?

____

____

____

c. Who was Amalek?

____

____

____

d. What did his nation represent?

____

____

____

Through God's direction Moses instructed Joshua to the lead the Israelites in battle against the Amalekites.

a. What were God's instructions for Moses regarding his part in the battle?

____

____

____

b. What happened when Moses grew tired?

____

____

____

c. Who came to Moses aid?

d. What does the rod of God represent?

e. What was the significance of God's rod being held up over the battlefield?

f. How did the Israelites gain victory on the battlefield?

g. What would have happened if Moses hadn't listened to God's direction?

Prayer is an essential part of the armor of God. It is critical that we spend time with God in prayer before we enter the battlefield.

a. Why can't we use the same defensive strategy that worked in our last battle?

b. Why are past victories good?

____

____

____

c. How can they become detrimental to our Christian walk?

____

____

____

In Paul's letter to the Ephesians he explains to them that they must be imitators of God and follow His example.

a. Who was God's example?

____

____

____

b. How was Jesus prayer life an example to us?

____

____

____

c. How can we be in a constant attitude of prayer?

____

____

____

d. According to John 11:41-42, how often does God hear our prayers?

____

____

____

e. According to Romans 8:34 what is Jesus doing on our behalf?

___

___

___

f. What does it mean to be attentive?

___

___

___

g. When we come to the Father in prayer, what do we receive?

___

___

___

h. What promise does God give us in Job 22:27-30?

___

___

___

We need to be watchful not only for ourselves but for those around us who are in need of prayer.

a. In the story of the paralytic, how did his friends intercede on his behalf?

___

___

___

b. Why couldn't they get to Jesus the conventional way?

___

___

___

c. How did they finally get their friend before Jesus?

____

____

____

d. What did Jesus do when He saw their faith?

____

____

____

e. What would have happened to the young paralytic if his friends gave up?

____

____

____

f. How can we take this story and apply it to our lives?

____

____

____

During Paul's incarceration he had opportunity to witness the Roman soldiers practicing their battle formations and various strategic moves.

a. How can we apply in the spiritual realm what the soldiers did with their shields?

____

____

____

b. How does prayer strengthen our armor as well as the armor of those around us?

____

____

____

c. How do we receive God's wisdom and discernment?

d. Think back on a time when you were *'Aaron or Hur'* to someone in your life. How did you show your support to them?

e. Think back on a time when you were *'Moses'* how did the *'Aaron & Hur'* of your life help and support you?

Study Guide – Chapter Nine

Armed In Deity

As soldiers in God's army we have been called, anointed and equipped with the spiritual armor that empowers us to stand against the devil with all his strategies and deceit.

a. How did Paul compare the physical armor of a soldier to the spiritual armor of God?

____

____

____

b. In Romans 13:14 what does Paul tell us to put on?

____

____

____

c. What does the phrase *'put on'* mean?

____

____

____

d. How do we clothe ourselves with truth?

____

____

____

e. Who is Truth?

____

____

____

In Paul's first letter to the Christians in Corinth he explains to them that it is through God that we have our life in Christ.

a. According to John 6:44 how do we come to Christ?

____

____

____

b. According to 1 Corinthians 1:30, who is our righteousness?

____

____

____

c. According to Ephesians 4:24 whose nature are we to put on?

____

____

____

We are taking on His attributes and His characteristics that we may represent Him to this world with excellence.

a. According to Colossians 3:12-14 what behavior is typical of Jesus Christ?

____

____

____

b. In this verse we are instructed to put on love. Who is love?

____

____

____

c. What is to rule and reign in our hearts?

____

____

____

The next part of Jesus character that God wants us to clothe ourselves in is that of faith.

a. According to Revelation 19:11 what is Jesus called?

____

____

____

b. When we put on faith what are we clothing ourselves with?

____

____

____

Salvation is a garment that God has so graciously clothed us in. When we put on salvation, here again we are clothing ourselves or immersing ourselves into the Lord Jesus Christ.

a. What does Jesus name mean?

____

____

____

b. As our covering, Jesus is both our _______________ and _________________.

c. According to John 1:1 how is Jesus described?

____

____

____

d. In the book of Revelation Jesus is called the Word of God. In Revelation 19:15 what is coming out of His mouth?

____

____

____

We must understand that Jesus is not only the personification of the aforementioned armor He is also our prayer warrior.

a. According to Hebrews 7:25 what is Jesus ever living to do?

____

____

____

b. What does Paul mean when he instructs us to put on the armor of Light?

____

____

____

c. Prior to their fallen state what was Adam and Eve's covering?

____

____

____

d. What is the definition of the word *'covering'*?

____

____

____

e. How does John describe Jesus in John 1:4?

____

____

____

f. How does Jesus describe Himself in John 8:12?

____

____

____

g. Our spiritual clothing is to be layered with __________, _______________, ____________, ___________, ____________________, ________________, and ________________.

h. Whose likeness and image have we been created in?

____

____

____

i. What does it mean to be armed in Deity?

____

____

____

j. How have we been made more than conquerors?

____

____

____

k. How have we gained a surpassing victory?

____

____

____

Jesus Christ is the armor of God. He is the covering God has instructed us to clothe ourselves in. We are to put on the Lord Jesus Christ and all His attributes so that we may successfully stand against the devil and all his cohorts. Through Him we are both **ARMED AND VICTORIOUS!**

Notes

[i] Strong's Exhaustive Concordance of the Bible written by James Strong, S.T.D, LL.D.

[ii] Strong's Exhaustive Concordance of the Bible written by James Strong, S.T.D, LL.D.

[iii] Merriam-Webster Online Dictionary © 2004 by Merriam Webster, Incorporated

[iv] Merriam-Webster Online Dictionary © 2004 by Merriam Webster, Incorporated

[v] Merriam-Webster Online Dictionary © 2004 by Merriam Webster, Incorporated

[vi] Merriam-Webster Online Dictionary © 2004 by Merriam Webster, Incorporated

[vii] UNRV History-Roman Weapons © 2003-2004 www.UNRV.com

[viii] Sparkling Gems from the Greek © 2003 by Rick Renner

[ix] Strong's Exhaustive Concordance of the Bible written by James Strong, S.T.D, LL.D.

[x] Merriam-Webster Online Dictionary © 2004 by Merriam Webster, Incorporated

[xi] Strong's Exhaustive Concordance of the Bible written by James Strong, S.T.D, LL.D.

[xii] Merriam-Webster Online Dictionary © 2004 by Merriam Webster, Incorporated

[xiii] Strong's Exhaustive Concordance of the Bible written by James Strong, S.T.D, LL.D.

[xiv] Strong's Exhaustive Concordance of the Bible written by James Strong, S.T.D, LL.D.

[xv] Strong's Exhaustive Concordance of the Bible written by James Strong, S.T.D, LL.D.

[xvi] Strong's Exhaustive Concordance of the Bible written by James Strong, S.T.D, LL.D.

[xvii] Strong's Exhaustive Concordance of the Bible written by James Strong, S.T.D, LL.D.

[xviii] Strong's Exhaustive Concordance of the Bible written by James Strong, S.T.D, LL.D.

[xix] Strong's Exhaustive Concordance of the Bible written by James Strong, S.T.D, LL.D.

[xx] Strong's Exhaustive Concordance of the Bible written by James Strong, S.T.D, LL.D.

[xxi] Moffatt New Translation of the New Testament

[xxii] Merriam-Webster Online Dictionary © 2004 by Merriam Webster, Incorporated

[xxiii] Strong's Exhaustive Concordance of the Bible written by James Strong, S.T.D, LL.D.

[xxiv] Strong's Exhaustive Concordance of the Bible written by James Strong, S.T.D, LL.D.

[xxv] Strong's Exhaustive Concordance of the Bible written by James Strong, S.T.D, LL.D.

[xxvi] Strong's Exhaustive Concordance of the Bible written by James Strong, S.T.D, LL.D.